The Life and Legacy of Gokhan Acikkollu

A Teacher Tortured to Death

as told by his wife
Mumine Tulay Acikkollu

written by
Mina Leyla

edited by
Hafza Girdap

AST PUBLISHING

The Life and Legacy
of
Gokhan Acikkollu

A Teacher Tortured to Death

Copyright © AST Publishing, 2022

All publication rights of this work belong to Advocates of Silenced Turkey. All rights reserved. No part of this book may be reproduced or transmitted in any form or by any means, electronic or mechanical, including photocopying, recording or by any information storage and retrieval system without permission in writing from the Advocates of Silenced Turkey.

www.silencedturkey.org

Published: August 2022
ISBN: 9798843025199

Fear is contagious, so is courage!

CONTENTS

About the Hizmet movement	5
Editor's Note	6
Preface	9
Foreword	15
The light of my life, Istanbul!	19
July 15th: Our son's birthday… Once the dearest day to us!	35
Hearts… Eyes… Ears	53
Country roads, take me home… to the place I belong!	64
Seeking justice, by any means necessary…	136
Even if the wind blows forever, the mountain never shakes!	222
A fresh start or an inevitable ending?	254
Life of Gokhan Acikkollu in chronological order	283
Photos	284
Violations of the Turkish Penal Code	292

The Life and Legacy of Gokhan Acikkollu

ABOUT THE HIZMET MOVEMENT

Hizmet is a transnational civil society initiative that advocates for the ideals of human rights, equal opportunity, democracy, non-violence, and the emphatic acceptance of religious and cultural diversity. This widespread movement began in Turkey as a grassroots community in the 1970s in the context of social challenges being faced at the time: violent conflicts among ideologically and politically driven youth, desperate economic conditions, and decades of a state-imposed ideology of discrimination that mandated a particular lifestyle.

Over the years, Hizmet has transformed from a grassroots community in Turkey to a much wider global effort with participants from all walks of life. Their work is centered upon promoting philanthropy and community service, investing in education to cultivate virtuous individuals, organizing intercultural and interfaith dialogue events to promote a peaceful coexistence.

Hizmet participants are inspired by the ideas and example of Fethullah Gulen, a Muslim scholar who has expressed the belief that serving fellow humans is as serving God.

For more information: www.afsv.org

EDITOR'S NOTE

Advocates of Silenced Turkey (AST) is a non-governmental organization that runs its activities on a voluntary basis since 2018. The aim of AST is to bring before international public opinion the human rights violations including torture and the unlawful court trials and proceedings, which have been encountered in Turkey especially the last ten years. After 2016, more than 160,000 innocent people lost their jobs in both public and private sectors, with accusations and unjust convictions of being connected with the coup attempt. The state of emergency, which was announced on July 20, 2016, gave the government unchecked powers - in the disguise of combatting terrorism - to persecute thousands of people with no accountability and to undermine the fundamental principles of a democratic society and the most basic principles of universal human rights and values such as freedom of expression and freedom of the press. Today, tens of thousands of highly qualified professionals such as judges, prosecutors, doctors, teachers, journalists, academics, and military officers have been detained and imprisoned in Turkey due to bogus terrorism charges. Around 5,000 of them are women, along with nearly 345 children who stay with their mothers in prisons. Hundreds of thousands of people have little or no hope of surviving the grueling atmosphere in Turkey, and as they are banned from leaving the country, they have no other choice but to flee at the risk of losing their lives by crossing the borders via dangerous routes. Some of them have not survived this difficult journey.

As the Advocates of Silenced Turkey, we engage in a number of activities in order not to keep silent about the injustices that have been taking place in Turkey where the rule of law has been suspended for a long time.

APH (Archiving the Persecution of Hizmet) project of recording and archiving the testimonies of victims, aims to shed light on the injustices suffered by thousands of people in Turkey. Our volunteers have conducted hundreds of interviews and thanks to their efforts, the victimizations, and hardships that the victims experienced are now being recorded in both spoken and written formats. The main purpose of this project is to ensure that these tragic stories are not allowed to fade into oblivion but are rather recorded accurately and impartially to leave firsthand sources for future generations. We also aim to bring this persecution to the attention of academics, media organizations, human rights associations, prominent community leaders, and government representatives at the international level.

"The Life and Legacy of Gokhan Acikkollu" is the product of a long-term endeavor. We would like to thank everyone who made tireless and valuable contributions to this work. We wish that Turkey will soon transform into a democratic society in which fundamental values like universal human rights and the rule of law are duly observed.

The Life and Legacy of Gokhan Acikkollu

PREFACE

When I watched the video footage showing the death of Gokhan Acikkollu in his cell for the first time, I was shaken to my core and thought to myself "Oh no! I wish his family won't see this!" Later on, when I was interviewing his wife Tulay, I learned that it was indeed her who had given that video footage to *BOLD Media* to be published. She had taken that footage from her husband's court file, but for a long time she didn't dare to watch it. As a matter of fact, she had watched it for the first time on the website of *BOLD Media*, and later on she watched the last moments of her husband hundreds of times, again and again!

Gokhan Acikkollu, a history teacher, is the first martyr of the Hizmet Movement after the controversial July 15 coup plot. All his lifetime, he had not known any other path than education, he had devoted himself to his students, to the extent that he was even neglecting his own family sometimes. Being in love with Istanbul, history, and his students, Gokhan had such a sweet and naïve personality. Actually, when he was performing his mandatory military service, his psychology got deteriorated just because he had to carry a rifle around every day and he started anxiety treatment.

It is so interesting and tragic that Gokhan Acikkollu was declared a terrorist just because one of his friends gave his name to the police while that same person was being tortured in custody. On July 23, 2016, in the middle of the night, around 20 police officers raided Gokhan's house, beat him and then took him into custody. The torture started that night and continued for the next 13 consecutive days. One of his ribs was broken when a police officer kicked him in the chest while he was taken from his home. In the following days, they tortured him nonstop. Whenever he was taken to a medical check, he talked to the doctors about the torture that he was exposed to. He was staying together with other four people in a cell of only 60 square feet, and he told his cellmates the details of the torture that he was going through every day. His cellmates couldn't do anything to prevent the torture. And when it comes to the police officers and the doctors around…well, they were quite remorseless.

Gokhan's heart just couldn't take all that torture anymore and it stopped on August 5, right before the sunrise. When he died, his official police statement was not even taken, yet. Despite this, the government attempted to bury him in the so-called and newly started "Cemetery of Traitors", without a funeral. Then they allowed his family to take his dead body, but they didn't allow them to bury him within the boundaries of Istanbul. His wife's family transported his body in their own car to Konya, 700 kilometers away from Istanbul. The family was not provided a proper coffin, neither an *imam* had led his funeral prayer.

One and a half years after his death, the government reinstated him to his job! Yes, one and a half years AFTER his death! Of course, his murderers will be held accountable in the Hereafter, if not in this world. His dear wife Tulay is seeking for justice and says that "courage is contagious, just like fear is." She emphasizes that it is not vengeance that she is after, it is justice: "*All that matters for me is that one day when justice comes, those left behind will have a piece of relief. And those who oppressed innocent people will have their courage and arrogance broken. When the stories of the oppression is told loud enough for the entire world to hear it, perhaps there wouldn't be any new government plots like the one of "July 15" and there wouldn't be new victims. That is my only concern.*

Otherwise, if the troubles that the oppressors will have in this world will lessen their punishment in the Hereafter, I want them to live here with full comfort. Let them enjoy this world. Let my heart won't find comfort in this world! That's all right. Because I know that there is a Hereafter. I know that those oppressors will face the eternal justice and penalty there.

They very well know how wrong and corrupted they are. On the other hand, we know that we are on the right side and we are so grateful and humble for that. And that realization alone is sufficient."

Tulay is one of the strongest women I have ever seen in my life. I have interviewed her for eight months in the process of writing this book. She was so kind to share her deepest and most intimate feelings with me. I wouldn't hesitate to bear witness that the Acikkollu family is indeed a beautiful family who has put *Hizmet* to the center of their lives. For them, serving people is serving God.

Gokhan was such a humble person who was not telling to anyone, not even to his wife, about the good deeds that he was doing. And apparently, God had blessed him with a wife who is as considerate as he was. When she had crossed the Maritza river with her children together to flee Turkey, they had walked several hours at the Greek side of the border. When they were passing through a small village in the middle of the night, being totally exhausted, Tulay saw a few plastic chairs left outside in front of a café. For a second, she thought to sit on the chair to rest a little but then quickly changed her mind, because, she said to me later in the interview, that *"it wouldn't be appropriate for us to sit on those chairs without getting permission of the owner of the café."*

The Life and Legacy of Gokhan Acikkollu

Gokhan Acikkollu was an innocent citizen, a good son to his parents, an idealist teacher, a husband in love with his wife, a loving and caring father to his children, and a religious man of *Hizmet*. He lost his life due to persecution and negligence of the corrupted judicial system, media, police, and even medical doctors. His wife's pursuit of justice was tried to be blocked by a prosecutor's "decision of non-prosecution".

In this book, you will read the life story of Gokhan Acikkollu, as told by his wife Tulay and written by me. The interview process and the other related research has taken more than a year.

Hereby, I invite you to witness the life story of an innocent teacher who was tortured to death by the government.

While reading the book, please listen to your heart and conscience!

Mina Leyla

July 2022

We dedicate this work, which is based on true stories…
…to the thousands of people in Turkey, who have been deprived of their liberty and still face persecution.
…to innocent people who had to flee their homeland and get separated from their families.
…to all victims who have set out for a new life in which they just want to live freely without any further injustice.
…and to those who have lost all their hope of going back and living in their homelands.

We sincerely thank…
Mrs. Mumine Tulay Acikkollu
for sharing her story with AST
Our author Mina Leyla
Book Editor Hafza Girdap
Translators R.H., C.L, M.F.
English Editors Barbara W., Hande Hur
Illustrator B.H.
Cover Design Esranur Bozdemir
…and everyone else who contributed to this project.

The Life and Legacy of Gokhan Acikkollu

FOREWORD

In Pursuit of Justice

My name is Mumine Tulay Acikkollu. I had been married to Gokhan Acikkollu for twenty-two years… I am a witness to his innocence and sincerity both in this world and the Hereafter. That he was murdered by those who currently hold the government power won't change that fact. My husband Gokhan was taken into custody through an assault by twenty-five police officers raiding our home only a week after the so-called coup attempt of July 15, 2016 in Turkey. He was subjected to systemic torture for thirteen days in the Istanbul Vatan Police Precinct. He was also deprived of his prescribed drugs during that time.

He was fully cut off from us during this time, and we were told that even if we were to hire a lawyer, they would not allow Gokhan to see the lawyer. After almost two weeks and without even his statement being taken, he was murdered on August 5, 2016 under custody. When he died, there was no indictment whatsoever containing any information of any charge against him. Nonetheless, he was declared "guilty" to the public and was to be buried in the "traitor's cemetery."

A whole eighteen months after his death, he was reinstated to his job.

All my endeavors for justice after my husband's death came to grief. Two years after the so-called coup attempt I was summoned by the prosecutor's office. My kids and I were targeted by the government mouthpiece media and a court case was filed against me.

The Erdogan government who left my kids without a father had decided to continue their unending grudge against me. In order to keep my family together – with one dearest person missing – I made a hard decision: migrate to Greece by crossing the Maritza River. I chose freedom over captivity.

I currently work hard to hold onto life in a European country. Having started from scratch, I keep trying to look ahead for my children. I also made a promise: I will continue to seek justice for my husband until the end of my life. I will not relinquish. It is not revenge that I am seeking. I want justice! Since I believe that courage is contagious, just like fear.

All that matters for me is that one day when justice comes, those left behind will have a piece of relief. And those who oppressed innocent people will have their evil courage and arrogance broken. When the stories of the oppression is told loud enough for the entire world to hear it, perhaps there wouldn't be any new government plots like the one of "July 15" and there wouldn't be new victims. That is my only hope.

Otherwise, if the troubles that the oppressors will have in this world will lessen their punishment in the Hereafter, I want them to live here with full comfort. Let them enjoy this world. Let my heart won't find comfort in this world! That's all right. Because I know that there is a Hereafter. I know that those oppressors will face the eternal justice and penalty there.

They very well know how wrong and corrupted they are. On the other hand, we know that we are on the right side and we are so grateful and humble for that. And that realization alone is sufficient. Yes, they live in their palaces in this world. Suffering from extreme paranoia, they spend each night in a different one of the thousand rooms in their palace for security reasons, yet they will never attain the tranquility we carry in our hearts!

Who knows, one day we might sprout from where we were broken…

Chapter 1

The light of my life, Istanbul!

The light of my life, Istanbul!

HOW DEAR IS THE COLOR RED!

"The light of my life, Istanbul!" I suppose not too many people can personalize the city they love to that extent and express their attachment with such sincerity. Gokhan had a soft-hearted personality. He was born and raised in Istanbul and did not leave there until college. He had fallen in love with the city for which many poems and songs were written. But then again, that was Gokhan, his love was always deep and sincere. Besides, how could someone so passionate about history not love Istanbul anyhow? You can find Roman, Byzantine, and Ottoman ruins in every part of the city. Whenever you turn a corner, you come across a Roman epitaph or a Byzantine wall... or an Ottoman fountain might greet you.

Gokhan was born in the Sirinevler district of Istanbul to a homemaker mom and a teacher father, who were originally from the eastern Turkish city of Kars. The family had to leave Kars long ago due to the job of the grandfather as a customs officer. My father-in-law was only ten-years-old when they moved to Istanbul. He later married his cousin and kept Istanbul as their new home. Gokhan and all of his three younger siblings were born in Istanbul.

Gokhan's first and last family trip to Kars took place

when he was a fifth grader. Neither he nor any other member of his family went back to Kars again, not even for a short visit.

They lived in Istanbul, but they lived as a typical Anatolian family. Struggling as a family of six in that crowded metropolis on a teacher's salary, the parents couldn't provide enough guidance for their children's education to the extent that a visual disability Gokhan had since birth got noticed only by his teacher in elementary school.

He would later frequently talk about the time he had an operation on his eyes and say, "I understood how dear the color red was only after I had surgery. Until then I used to think everyone else saw red as blurry."

That surgery apparently was a turning point in his life. Before he was only mediocre in his classes, after the surgery he became a successful student once he could better see what is written on the blackboard and in the books.

As far as I know, as he grew up, there were times his family passed through certain hardships. For instance, once his father was assigned to a job in the city of Erzurum and had to leave his children with their uncle for some time. Another time, he needed to leave his job

The light of my life, Istanbul!

for a while due to some issues, and the family experienced serious financial turmoil.

Gokhan was not raised in a religiously observant family. Both parents were more like what one would call "cultural Muslims", they believed in God but were not practicing. My husband's religious views were shaped when he started high school and met with college students from the Hizmet movement. In his words, he was most impressed by their "selflessness." It was no surprise, because he himself had such an altruistic personality.

He was the eldest of his siblings and also the most devoted one to his parents. He would get very upset by even the smallest quarrel of his siblings with their parents and could not stand even the tiniest tribulation of them. I never recall him making his parents sad or causing any trouble to them. He used to always make sure that whatever we had in our house also was in his parent's house.

In the first few years of our marriage we were working in Nevsehir, a small Anatolian city. One day, when he was talking to his mom over the phone and learned that she had flu, he was deeply saddened. After hanging up, he sobbed, putting his head between his hands: "Mom is trying to survive the winter in a stove-heated house over there, whereas we live here in the comfort of central heating." I was surprised, and to be honest found it a bit odd. I asked, "What should we do?" and continued "Shall we also move into a stove-heated house? Why are you blaming yourself?" After all, we had been married only a few years ago and were trying to pay off our debts. We were in need of financial support and had no means to help them. However, he had such a tender heart: he would do whatever he could to fix a problem and would feel despair if he could not do anything about it.

He was deeply affectionate towards his parents. He loved his job as a history teacher...and of course he loved Istanbul. I recall from the years we were working in various towns of Anatolia: Whenever he saw a scene from Istanbul on TV, he used to sigh: "Istanbul! The light of my life!"

A TOMBOY

As soft and sensitive as Gokhan was, I was a girl brought up like a boy. I was born in the city of Konya to a worker father and a homemaker mother. I had an older sister, two older brothers and one younger brother. Being the only one among my siblings who had gone to college, my father was so proud of me.

The light of my life, Istanbul!

My father was not sent to school by his parents when he was a child. Having a chip on his shoulder about this, he always wanted his children to go to school. However, my brothers were not into school at all. My sister, on the other hand, very much wanted to go to college. She got even admitted to the School of Nursing in another city but when my father asked my grandmother whether she could live with my sister together in an apartment that he would rent so she could go to college, my grandma rejected the idea. She even responded furiously: "School is not a girl's place! I won't stay with her together and if you send her to college, I won't give my blessings to you forever." Sadly, that was the end of my sister's education journey. Hence, I was the only child going to college, and my father was overly affectionate towards me. When I was going to high school, every instance when my mom asked me to do some housework, my dad would intervene and say: "Don't disturb my daughter, she will go to college soon, she needs to study." He was always proud of me.

I didn't happen to be that stereotypical little girl who plays with dolls. My childhood friends were mostly my older brothers' friends, and my childhood game was mostly soccer. As is, I was a quarrelsome tomboy.

The Life and Legacy of Gokhan Acikkollu

I had gone to a boarding high school, specializing in health and hospitality services, and had a compulsory healthcare duty after high school due to my scholarship. Yet, I had always wished to become a teacher. Seeking that path, I applied to the School of Theology in Ankara and got admitted. The following years were very busy in college, attending classes in the daytime and working overnight shifts in the hospital.

Like Gokhan's, my family was also not familiar with the Hizmet movement. I had come to Ankara to register for my first classes in the college. As I was not assigned yet to work by the Ministry of Health, I couldn't stay in the housing units provided by the ministry. My father told me: "I have heard from some friends that apparently there are student houses of the Nur movement[1] in Ankara, we can try them!" Hearing this from my father, I immediately warmed to the idea and said: "I want to live in one of those student houses."

We had a visit to one of those houses and met with students living there. I had really liked the setting and this

---

1 A Sunni movement founded at the beginning of the twentieth century based on the writings of Said Nursi (1877–1960). He emphasized the importance of salvation in this world and the afterlife through education and freedom, the synthesis of Islam and science, and democracy as the best form of governance within the rule of law.

is how I started living in Hizmet houses. I had a character inclined to read and learn about religion. While looking for a book to read in that student house, I discovered the books of an author with the name Abdulfettah Sahin. I enjoyed reading several books of him. A roommate who realized that I loved reading suggested one day, "If you wish, you can dip into the books of Fethullah Gulen[2]." I was not taken by this suggestion and responded, "Thanks, but I like reading Abdulfettah Sahin and enjoy his style of writing. Maybe later I will have a look at the books of the author you just mentioned." She smiled that day. It took me a while to learn that both authors were, to my surprise, actually the same person: Abdulfettah Sahin was one of the pen names Gulen used.

DEPRIVED OF THE BEST YEARS OF OUR LIVES

It was called Zubeyde Hanim Maternity Hospital then. Later it was united with another hospital under a different

---

[2] Fethullah Gulen is an Islamic scholar, preacher and social advocate, whose decades-long commitment to education, altruistic community service, and interfaith harmony has inspired millions in Turkey and around the world. Described as one of the world's most important Muslim figures, Gulen has reinterpreted aspects of Islamic tradition to meet the needs of contemporary Muslims. He has dedicated his life to interfaith and intercultural dialogue, community service and providing access to quality education. For more information, please visit www.afsv.org

name. I spent my five years in Ankara attending classes in college during the day and having overnight work shifts in that hospital. All those years, I stayed in the student houses of the Hizmet Movement, made lots of dear friends and had a happy college life. We were happy around each other, however the country was going through a dark turmoil and we were deprived of the best years of our lives. The regime which nowadays labels us as "terrorists" just because of reading Quran, gathering in our houses, reading books, and giving charity to needy students, back then labeled us as "fundamentalists who try to topple the modern government with their *hijabs*[3]". We were only 18 to 22-year-old students whose only goal was to have a college degree. Alas! We couldn't explain ourselves to anyone...neither yesterday nor today.

There were only six nurses wearing *hijab* in the big hospital where I was working. We were working harder than anyone else around, but still we had to give a defense statement to the administration every week, just because we were wearing *hijab* while working. We were getting endless warnings for not following the so-called dress code of the hospital. We were so young, with beautiful

---

[3] Arabic word, refers to headcoverings worn by Muslim women. While Islamic headcoverings can come in many forms, hijab often specifically refers to a cloth wrapped around the head and neck, covering the hair but leaving the face visible.

minds, and it didn't matter to them that we were just some young girls who would never harm even an insect, let alone any human being.

We were even deprived of regular employee benefits. I still remember the day when I had requested to take 4 hours off by using some of my accumulated overtime hours. That was a usual practice that other employees were using every now and then. When I went to the head nurse's office and explained the situation, she responded: "Only if your mother were on her deathbed, I would let you off!"

My attitude in those tough times was to not consent to oppression, and I kept telling my other colleagues to not be demoralized and to look happy and strong when they entered the head nurse's office. I was telling them, "Hold your head high, smile, crack even some jokes here and there, don't bow down!"

Those were the days following the "February 28" post-modern coup in Turkey. Dark plots were being planned and executed by the regime to intimidate the ordinary citizens who were religious and especially those who were wearing *hijabs*. Some of those religious men and women whom we had considered our brothers and sisters in faith, those with whom we had together struggled against the oppression of the regime only 15 years ago have slowly turned into the worst tyrants themselves, much worse than before. How could we know this all? The oppressed ones of yesterday have become the cruel oppressors of today and got involved in the biggest corruption scandals in the history of Turkey.

Turkey was passing through economic hardships back then, too. Patients who were visiting our hospital without any health insurance were offered a deal behind the doors: if they were to file a complaint against the nurses wearing *hijabs*, they were discharged without any dues. "Was your midwife wearing a *hijab*?" or "Did the nurse who was taking care of you have a *hijab*?" If you would answer "Yes" to these kinds of questions and file a complaint, you could leave the hospital without paying any bills. Well, I couldn't get angry at those poor people who couldn't afford to pay their bills; they just saw the opportunity and took it. Still, this was what we had to go through during those difficult times.

TWO SOULS UNAWARE OF EACH OTHER

Gokhan went to Necip Fazıl Kısakurek High School in Istanbul, Bahcelievler. My high school was in Konya. Both of us had the same dream, though: becoming a teacher. Gokhan wanted to attend the FEM education center of Hizmet movement in Istanbul to prepare for the college entrance exams but his father had said, "Don't even dream about it; we can't afford the tuition cost of that place."

He had told me once how he worked in a printing office all sumer long to make money to cover the tuition of the education center. He had always talked about his persistence in those challenging days with pride. He had not despaired but was fully determined and got into college with his hard work. The year I got into the School of Theology in Ankara and left Konya, he had moved into my hometown to attend the History Department at Konya University. The year was 1993.

...

School of Theology was a five-year institution. When I was a senior, Gokhan had already graduated and started as a teacher in the Nevsehir Serhat Learning Center. We had not yet met.

If you ask, "How did your roads intersect?" my response would be, "The will of God." A close friend of mine was engaged to Gokhan's friend. They thought of us as being tailor-made for each other and suggested to introduce us to each other. I accepted.

It was a hot summer night in July when he called me for the first time, on the hospital's phone number. We were both shy. Our first conversations were pretty much like: "How many siblings do you have? Where does your family live? What do they do for living?" I had plans of visiting my sister in Istanbul during my annual leave in August. We planned to meet each other in person, in Istanbul.

It was August of 1997, but I honestly don't recall the exact date. We had arranged to meet in Bakirkoy Square. I went there with my sister. Quite thrilled, I was looking around for him. There he was, walking towards us with a smiling face, and a red rose in his hand. What was the rose for? It was definitely not a mark or sign that we had planned to meet, it was just a little gesture from him.

We walked for a while and sat at a table in a tea house. My sister left to give us some privacy. It was 25 years ago. We were not as relaxed then as today's young generation. Feeling shy to talk, we have first sneaked a couple of looks at each other. Then I broke the silence and asked directly: "What do you expect from a marriage?" His reply in a soft voice was brief and concise: "Love and respect." And then he continued: "Being happy together and sharing the same values." When he asked the same question to me, my answer was quick: "I want to establish a Hizmet house."

The light of my life, Istanbul!

Nowadays, that sentence alone is enough to be declared a "terrorist"(!); I had only meant: "I want a home, which would be filled with guests, in which we would not sit at the dinner table alone, in which we could raise our kids with the thought system of the *Risale-i Nur*[4], where we keep Qur'an and our prayers in the center of our daily lives, and where we live giving a hand to the needy people around and sharing our bread with them." That was the meaning of my sentence back then, and it still is.

We chatted for a long while at that table on our first meeting. Time flew by so fast. We left the table that day with warm feelings towards each other. It was a gift of God to unite our hearts. Not long after, my sister invited Gokhan and his family over for dinner. Both my sister and my brothers met with Gokhan and his family, and they approved our relationship. My parents also gave their approval and blessings. It was January of 1998 when we got engaged in Konya, Seydisehir. We got married after one year, in August 1998.

...

---

[4] Collection of the books written by Said Nursi. Rather than being a Quranic commentary which expounds all its verses giving the immediate reasons for their revelation and the apparent meanings of the words and sentences, the Risale-i Nur is a commentary which expounds the meaning of the Quranic truths. The verses mostly expounded in the Risale-i Nur are those concerned with the truths of belief, such as the divine names and attributes and the divine activity in the universe, the divine existence and unity, resurrection, Prophethood, divine determining or destiny, and man's duties of worship.

The Life and Legacy of Gokhan Acikkollu

Both of us were working. We wanted to cover all the wedding expenses ourselves and not put a burden on our families. Naturally, we got into some serious debt. Every young person dreams of a beautiful wedding. I must confess that ours was a disappointment. Back then, it was fashionable to arrange hymn orators in religious weddings. We had wished for such a simple but beautiful wedding but ended up in a low-class wedding house. Several hymns were played initially to possibly please us, but they soon shifted into folklore dances and local songs. The guests were having a good time for sure, but not us!

Gokhan had also felt distressed because of the ambience and when the time came for it, he didn't want to raise my bridal veil. The relatives from his and my side kept saying, "Open the bride's veil," but Gokhan evaded them all by responding, "It's good as is." Even when we cut our wedding cake and he passed a piece for me to taste, he paid attention as much as he could to not lift my veil all the way. Yet it was a very hot August day, and I was really sweltering under the veil. I couldn't resist telling him: "Gokhan, let me lift the veil, it's so hot." That was how I lifted my own veil in the wedding. Later, we kept laughing whenever we recalled those moments.

That's how our wedding was--all the relatives having a fun time, except us. Though it was not a big deal for either one of us. In the end, I was marrying "the man who shared the same values with me." We were fully supporting each other.

Chapter 2

July 15th: Our son's birthday...

Once the dearest day to us!

July 15th: Our son's birthday… Once the dearest day to us!

I WILL NEVER MARRY ANYONE WHO'S A THEOLOGIAN OR FROM KONYA!

My husband had often volunteered in the Hizmet movement during college, so he had interacted with a good number of theologists. Being a theologist, I can easily say that we have many graduates who have the most constant mindsets one can ever imagine. If I hadn't known Hizmet movement, most probably I would be such a person like them, too.

I personally heard many times from people: "No reasonable person comes out of Ankara Theology School." The name of the school suggests that religion is studied there and religious students are raised in it. However, a significant portion of the faculty were either atheist or deist. It was not unusual that students who started freshman year with *hijab* would not use *hijab* anymore when they were seniors. We had a constant struggle between conservatives and modernists in our school. If you hadn't joined one of the two camps, you had to straddle. I was among the ones who did so. With the perspective I attained from Nur and Hizmet philosophy, I was lucky enough to filter the education I was getting so as to refrain from anything extreme.

A delicate soul like Gokhan would be worn out in such

an environment where strong argumentative discussions were quite habitual. He had told me that before we met each other he had made up his mind: "I will never marry anyone who's a theologian or from Konya". Well, guess what! He eventually married me, a theologian from Konya!

...

We started to live in Nevsehir after the wedding. He was working in Serhat Learning Center, and I started to work in a community health center. Gokhan already had a network of friends. I met with their wives, so we became family friends. Most of us were newly married. We were getting together frequently and having a good time.

About a year after we got married, our son was born. My pregnancy was quite difficult. Our baby was diagnosed with Down syndrome, and I had to go alone all the way to Ankara for doctor visits due to Gokhan's busy work schedule. Gokhan had a heavy workload; he often used to call his students after he came home to follow up with their homeworks. Although it was difficult both physiologically and psychologically, I never complained about anything during my pregnancy. I knew why Gokhan could not give me enough time, so I had peace of mind.

The doctor I visited in Ankara wanted to get an amniocentesis test done, but I didn't consent to it. When

July 15th: Our son's birthday... Once the dearest day to us!

he warned me: "You might need to carry that burden through your whole life" my response was: "Only God would know that!" I was content with whatever God would give me as a trial. I definitely would not have taken my baby's right to life. Another doctor I visited had performed an ultrasound check and said that our baby didn't have Down syndrome. I was not fully relieved, though. It was really stressful for me to deal with such suspicions while going through other health problems.

However, I was able to stay patient and get ready for whatever God wished for us. Right after the delivery, while still feeling the pains of labor, I immediately asked to see my baby. He was a perfect little boy!

JULY 15TH: ONCE THE DEAREST DAY TO US...!

That was the happiest and dearest day of our lives. Contrary to the health screenings in pregnancy, our son was born perfectly healthy. We named him "Murat Fatih." Why? Gokhan's beloved grandfather Murat had passed away about two years before we got married. Gokhan had decided then that if he had ever a son, he would name him after his grandfather. Besides, as a history teacher he was a staunch fan of Fatih Sultan Mehmed, the Conqueror. When he told me that it was always his dream to name his son Murat Fatih, I responded half-jokingly, "What about my dreams?" Honestly, I was thinking of the name "Bera" who was a companion of the Prophet. I didn't want to disappoint him so I gave up my dream.

July 15th, 1999… It was like a holy day for us. We were able to have our baby in our arms. He was such a healthy boy despite we were told so many times during the pregnancy that he would have health issues. July 15 was a day of happiness and joy, and it stayed like that for the next seventeen years, until 2016.

…

The year our Murat Fatih was born, some other family friends also had their first babies born. While we were taking care of our children, we were often preparing *manti*[5] and *borek*[6] for fundraisers organized for needy students.

Activities which would nowadays make us declared as "terrorists" (!) were good deeds we raced for, back then. We used to visit student houses, ask for their needs, and offer our help for anything they demanded. As he grew

---
5   *Manti* is a type of dumpling popular in the Turkish cuisine. The dumplings typically consist of a spiced meat mixture, usually lamb or ground beef, in a thin dough wrapper and either boiled or steamed. Served with a yogurt and butter sauce.
6   *Borek* is made of a thin flaky dough such as filo with a variety of fillings, such as meat, cheese, spinach or potatoes.

July 15th: Our son's birthday... Once the dearest day to us!

up, my son Fatih became like a mascot for the college students living in those student houses. I remember when he was three, he didn't want to visit the student houses with me anymore. He was getting shy that the college girls were asking him to pronounce "wardrobe" and then laughing at him.

We had settled down a bit, but Gokhan still had to perform the mandatory military service. As we saw it as a duty to our country, it was important for us. In August of 2002, Gokhan departed to Hakkari Semdinli to join the military, leaving us in Nevsehir. He would come after 7 months, in March of the following year. Although he could, he didn't use any leave days during his military service. He would rather finish the service earlier. It was very difficult to travel between Semdinli and Nevsehir anyhow. He had to change several buses and it was taking such a long time.

We were all nervous due to high terror incidents in his military service area. We relied on God. For seven months long, I was not able to visit him and neither could he come to visit us. I was still working and taking care of a toddler meanwhile, it was almost impossible for me to visit him, anyhow. The roads in that area were not very safe, either. Every now and then he got a chance to call us from a payphone, so we would be able to hear each other's voices. Unfortunately, Gokhan couldn't cope well with all the stress due being so far away from his family, so he was diagnosed with anxiety. Whatever he had seen and lived through there had incited psychological disorders such as panic attacks. He was telling us that he had an anxiety disorder and started using antidepressants. Guard duties, the stress of daily musters, carrying a rifle every day…none of these was fitting his personality. A doctor we later visited told us it was not uncommon for men who had to stay away from their families to develop such disorders. Thankfully, after a while, he was assigned to give history lectures in the learning center of the military. That relieved him a bit. He was into teaching with pens, definitely not into weapons.

As I was trying to console my husband, I also was observing the psychological developments of our three-year-old. He was furious at his dad, as he was thinking his daddy had left us. Once he picked a photo out of our family album in which I was alone and cried out, hugging it, "Why has daddy left us? Why did he leave mommy alone…?" He was quite emotional, like a copy of his father. He still is, but now he prefers to hide his feelings.

…

It was the beginning of March; the doorbell rang in the evening. We didn't know when Gokhan would return, so we didn't even think about that possibility

July 15th: Our son's birthday… Once the dearest day to us!

when we heard the doorbell ringing. I thought it must be the doorkeeper of the building who walks through the apartments for the daily evening service. When I opened the door, I was shocked: Gokhan was standing right in front of me. When my son saw his father, he angrily turned his back and ran to the bedroom. I was screaming with joy and excitement.

When I saw Gokhan after so many months, with his military haircut, it first felt odd. In the following days whenever I looked at his hairstyle, I smiled. It took a couple of days for us, me and our son, to get used to the "new Gokhan." Fatih didn't even want to speak with his dad for several days.

A MAN IN LOVE WITH HIS JOB

We stayed a couple of months in Nevsehir after Gokhan returned home from military service. When Gokhan found a job as a middle school principal in Aksaray Sabah Learning Center, we had to move to Aksaray in the beginning of the summer. That same year I applied for a teaching position in public schools. The health care sector was getting more and more tiring for me. Being a teacher was my dream job and I could spend more time with my son, too.

We started to live in Aksaray in the summer of 2003. However, my appointment as religious studies teacher was approved only by April of 2004. Moreover, my appointment was in a different city, Hatay, instead of Aksaray. My son and I temporarily moved to Hatay, and thankfully after a couple of months, I was able to move back to Aksaray through the family union process.

Gokhan was always busy. In Nevsehir, he used to work both as a branch principal and as a teacher. Here in Aksaray he had only an administrative job, but somehow he was busier. He was leaving home very early and coming back quite late. Even when he was home, he was still occupied with following up on his students. He used to call them to get their daily study reports. I had a more flexible schedule. Well, that meant that I had to take care of most of the responsibilities at home, to the extent that I was usually the one who was fixing things when something was broken at home.

We were not even spending time outside the home as a family. I don't remember having a family picnic, neither in Nevsehir nor in Aksaray. We used to have field trips and picnics with students or have events with friends, but not just as a family. It was only after so many years when we moved back to Istanbul that we were able to have a family picnic. You might think that I complain about all

July 15th: Our son's birthday... Once the dearest day to us!

this as I narrate them now. No, not at all! On the contrary, I never complained about it, not even once. My husband and I were sharing a dream together, an ideal... a path to follow. We were racing in doing good deeds without expecting anything in return. That was our path. And of course, it required a lot of sacrifice. Yes, sometimes it was difficult not to be able to spend some family time together, but I knew that Gokhan loved me and our son very much.

Time was passing by, our son was growing up, and we were busy with our jobs. Meanwhile, I had two miscarriages in those years. This is why I always have had mixed feelings for Aksaray. We stayed three years there, between 2003 and 2006. Then we moved to Konya, my hometown, and settled in there.

"YOUR BABY'S SURVIVAL CHANCE IS TEN PERCENT!"

In June 2006, I was appointed to Konya. We moved in July. Gokhan was appointed to the Mevlana branch of Hizmet-affiliated learning centers in downtown Konya. He was always busy until then, but this time my schedule was getting quite busy, too. In addition to my job in the school, we used to organize seminars and fundraising activities with my friends in Hizmet.

As both of us were busy, we saw each other for only short periods of time in a typical day. It was seldom that both of us managed to come home early. If that happened, as a family activity we would watch a TV series, meanwhile enjoying some potato chips and chocolate bars. Somehow we managed to finish all the seasons of the series Fringe and Lost, which were quite popular at that time. Gokhan was the chocolate monster of home. I was suspecting that he had diabetes, but he used to pass it off. I kept insisting, "You sweat a lot, you go to restroom frequently. You eat lots of desserts. Please let's go and get a blood work," but he never wanted to.

…

Our son was turning ten. I was again pregnant after two miscarriages. And again, doctors were not quite promising. They said "The baby has only ten percent chance of survival. Be ready for anything. If the baby's heartbeat stops, we will abort the baby." I had to stay in the hospital for three and a half months. I was drinking six liters of water every day. I used to recite all the prayers I know of and ask God to grant us a healthy baby. There were some days Gokhan couldn't stay with me during that time period. I had never wished for a special attention

July 15th: Our son's birthday… Once the dearest day to us!

anyhow. Actually, I wanted that he wouldn't neglect his students and we could give due attention to our students.

Our daughter, who we were told only had a ten percent possibility of surviving, was born on August 13th, 2009 as a premature baby. She was nine weeks early and had lung complications. My husband wanted to name her "Munise" as suggested by someone he respected very much. My son and I liked the name "Zeynep" so we named her "Zeynep Munise."

The pregnancy was tough, but the time period after her birth was even tougher. Zeynep Munise stayed in newborn intensive care unit for 66 days. I had to stay in the hospital for one and a half months, both for my health, and also for our daughter's. As an infection carried over from the uterus, my leg developed thrombosis. It also caused clotting in my liver, and I had to use very strong medications for that. I was not able to nurse the baby during that time period. Mother's milk is the best for a baby, but our only option was formula feeding. I had to pump my milk out and pour it off to the sink. I can't express how hurtful this was, both physically and mentally.

How could I have known back then that many years later thousands of innocent young mothers to be imprisoned due to a staged coup attempt? They too had to pour their milk into the sink because they were not allowed to nurse their babies due to a crime they never committed. After learning about such persecutions, I kept remembering those painful memories from my past.

Those were the days of trouble… Every day, doctors were coming up with something new. One day they would say, "She has trouble hearing." Another day they would say, "She had too much oxygen therapy for so long. She might experience mental development issues in the future." I was really getting stressed out as I heard those words every other day.

After 66 days my daughter was discharged. We had to bring many different devices to home for her health problems. For one year, we kept visiting the doctors frequently, whose pessimistic scenarios never ceased to end. After so many tests related to her hearing, eyesight and mental development we finally were fully convinced that she was a normal baby. Thanks be to God!

GOKHAN REJOINS HIS LOVE: ISTANBUL

As I said before, Gokhan was in love with Istanbul. To be honest, I was frightened by that huge metropolis. This is why while he was overjoyed when he was told about an

July 15th: Our son's birthday... Once the dearest day to us!

open position in a private school in Istanbul, I was not really into it. I guess he had prayed very sincerely to get that job because soon we got appointed to Istanbul. So we moved again, this time to Istanbul. It was August of 2010.

Gokhan had started in one of the branches of Doga Schools. However, he could endure there only for six months. The attitude of teachers, students, and even parents was quite different than what we were familiar with when we were living in Anatolia. He couldn't find the warmth and sincerity in the school community he used to have in his previous schools. So, he decided to transfer to Hizmet's Ufuk High School in Istinye. We were living in Umraniye, and he had to commute to Istinye every day. I was working at Umraniye Mediha Tansel Middle School.

About a year after we moved to Istanbul, Gokhan took the KPSS[7] test just to see how he would perform. He didn't have the intention to leave the Hizmet schools; but since his test score was quite good, he applied for some open positions. I have to admit that both the kids

---

7 Abbreviation for *Kamu Personeli Secme Sinavi* in Turkish, Public Personnel Selection Examination, is used in Turkey for determining the people who will be assigned as civil servants for the first time. Civil servant candidates can begin their professional career depending on the scores they get from this exam. It measures general ability, general culture skills and formation knowledge of civil servant candidates.

and I were extremely happy that he could get into a public school. We used to see each other not much when he was working in the private schools. He was leaving home very early, coming late in the night, and spending all his time and energy for the institution that he was working for. He felt an even heavier burden of responsibility when he had administrative positions.

Had this very busy schedule ever been an issue among us? As I indicated before, I always respected his efforts and shared his ideals and goals. As a woman who attended both high school and college away from her family, I knew how to take care of myself and stand on my feet. Wherever he couldn't put enough effort in, I made up for him and didn't let any problems arise. In the end, we had the same ideals and didn't have time to relax and procrastinate from our goals. As a matter of fact, I remember that several times, electricity and water services were disconnected in our house simply because Gokhan had forgotten to pay the bills. On the other hand, if something was related to his students and job, he wouldn't forget a single detail. He was very diligent and didn't have any tolerance for negligence in his job.

…

Gokhan got appointed by the Ministry of Education

July 15th: Our son's birthday... Once the dearest day to us!

to a school in Gaziantep in February 2012. I was still working in Istanbul, and the kids were going to school. So we didn't plan on moving as a family. This separation was not as hard as military service. We had the opportunity to talk to each other in video chat every day. He was also visiting us biweekly. Despite being far away, we passed these months relatively in comfort. He came to Istanbul frequently during that year he worked in Gaziantep. However, I didn't visit him with the kids, and I don't know why. I wish I would have done so, it would be nice to see that part of the country. Maybe we were so focused on him visiting us, that it never dawned on me to go and visit him.

He worked in Gaziantep Sehit Kamil High School for one year. He liked both the city and his students. As someone who likes desserts, it was not surprising that he was pleased to fall into the center of *baklavas*[8] and *katmers*[9]. It was also the first time he had to do housework by himself. Whenever he visited us in Istanbul, I was noticing that his whites turned into purplish colors. Like any man, I suppose, he was probably unaware that whites were supposed to be washed separately! He was possibly

---

[8] *Baklava* is a layered pastry dessert made of filo pastry, filled with chopped nuts, and sweetened with syrup or honey.
[9] *Katmer* is a traditional Turkish pastry made by baking folded layers of dough.

thinking, "Well, it gets cleaned, that's what matters!"

…

Gokhan returned home after a whole year. He got appointed to Umraniye Ataturk Anatolian High School. Some graduates of the middle school that I was working in were attending that high school, so we knew the same students.

Only a few years later, my husband was arrested like a ferocious "terrorist"(!) and tortured to death under custody. Please allow me to tell you a story which would be enough to explain what kind of personality he had: One of his student's family had recently moved from a small town in Anatolia to Istanbul. That student had learning disabilities, he had difficulties in expressing himself. As a result, his relationship with other students and even teachers was not great. He was my student in sixth grade and I was trying to help him through special education and guidance counseling. However, when he became a student of Gokhan in high school, that was when he made a significant progress. My husband paid extra special attention to him every day.

When I say "significant progress" you might think that I am saying this to praise my husband. That's not the case. Because these are not my words, rather they are

July 15th: Our son's birthday… Once the dearest day to us!

the words of the mother of that student. After Gokhan passed away, that student's mom had contacted me. With tears, she had expressed her feelings: "May God be pleased with Gokhan! He always helped and protected my son. When no one else wanted to have any relationship with him, it was our dear teacher Gokhan who took care of my son."

That was the Gokhan I have known. That was his character. He never withheld any support from his students; materially or morally. He wouldn't also talk about the good deeds that he was doing. Even I wouldn't know them, we used to learn about them from others, and only after some time had passed.

Chapter 3

Hearts... Eyes... Ears

Surely, among the jinn and humankind are many that We have created (and destined for) Hell (knowing that they would deserve it). They have hearts with which they do not seek the essence of matters to grasp the truth, and they have eyes with which they do not see, and they have ears with which they do not hear. They are like cattle (following only their instincts) rather, even more astray (from the right way and in need of being led). Those are unmindful and heedless.

Quran, chapter Araf, verse 179

Hearts... Eyes... Ears

A NUTELLA MONSTER AT HOME...

Nevsehir, Aksaray, Konya, İstanbul and Gaziantep... then Istanbul again. We were finally together as a family in the city that Gokhan was in love with. Having settled in, we were living all together with our son and daughter.

Gokhan loved his family and Istanbul, well he also loved tea and Nutella, actually all kinds of desserts. We usually watched movies together on the weekends, got up late on Sunday mornings, and liked to enjoy breakfasts which used to take hours. My husband, like most Turkish individuals, was a man with the ability to finish a pot of tea by himself. There were no quarrels in our family, actually most of the arguments we had were about Nutella. Even though my son Fatih and my daughter Zeynep were hiding all the jars in the house, it was futile; Gokhan would find them and already finish half the jar by the time we caught him. Especially if I was at school and if it was his day off, Nutella jars didn't stand a chance.

When Gokhan came home from school, my daughter would run in front of us and open the door. She would jump into her father's arms right away. One day, she smelled her father and asked, "You've eaten jelly beans, haven't you?" Gokhan whispered to our daughter with the guilt of being captured: "Don't tell mom, OK?" Of course, I had already heard it. But Zeynep didn't keep quiet anyhow and yelled at her dad, "Why didn't you bring me jelly beans, why?" We were all laughing.

Some days of the week Gokhan was picking up our daughter from school. When that was the case, they would return home usually with a toy. And they would hide it behind their backs so I wouldn't get angry. When they were together, they were like two kids. If a guest were to come to our house or if I was going to clean the house, I would kick them out. They didn't mind that, if anything they loved it. My husband had a Cinemaximum card, they would go to the movie theaters and not come home for hours because they loved watching two movies in a row.

As much as Munise Zeynep looked like me, Murat Fatih was just like a copy of his father. He took after his father in his sensitive and quiet personality, he was also a real tech-savvy guy, just like his father. He had attended International Olympiad in Informatics and got a bronze medal in the "Web Design" competition. Being so fond of informatics, it was not a surprise that he wanted to study computer engineering in college. But after July 2016, like everyone else, my son would learn to shelve his dreams and decide to attend the law school. After his father was murdered, he transferred from science major to the social studies major in his high school senior year.

Hearts... Eyes... Ears

In addition to his technological skills, our son also inherited cataracts genetically from his father. Just like when Gokhan was a child, cataracts had developed in Fatih's eyes, and he had a surgery when he was in the fifth grade.

It wouldn't be an exaggeration to call Gokhan a "tech monster" as well as a "dessert monster." Although, as a historian, he had a social sciences degree, he was as skilled in the world of electronics as a technician. His friends, when they would buy computers, phones, etc., would always consult with him. He was very interested in technological products, but especially in those from Apple. Whenever I was to get angry at him for wasting a lot of money on these things, he'd shut me down by saying, "That's my only luxury." Cables were gushing all over the house. TV set, laptop, desktop, speakers, headphones, phones, tablets, and everything else that had just come out was in our house. I was pretty uncomfortable with it and sometimes muttered my discontent. My excuse was ready. I'd say, "There's so much static electricity in the house, and this is why I am angry."

WE LEARN ABOUT GOKHAN'S DIABETES

Despite having worked in the health service area for more than ten years, I could not convince Gokhan to have a check-up. His excessive sweet addiction, sweating too much and frequent use of restroom pointed to diabetes, but he had kept saying for a long time: "I'm fine."

In 2014 he went on a tour to Europe with his friends. One of his friends, a doctor, convinced him to go to his office for a test, when they return to Turkey. Shortly after the test he got a call from his friend. He told Gokhan, "If you are standing, you need to sit down now!" According to the test results, his blood sugar values were so high that Gokhan could have a diabetic coma anytime.

To tell the truth, whenever he was home, he would not sit on a chair or sofa, he would rather lie down on the sofa. Most probably he was feeling weak due to diabetes. The doctor had said, "A weight of 10 kilos that a normal person carries feels like 100 kilos for someone who has diabetes."

Perhaps Gokhan was afraid to hear about the bad news, and that is why he hadn't been to the doctor all this time. Now he had to pay attention to his diet, use insulin, and exercise regularly. I'd say the entire year of 2015 was spent between home, school, and hospital. We bought a treadmill for home following the suggestion of the doctor, but I think my son used it more than Gokhan.

When he wasn't paying much attention to his diet, he was feeling fatigue and foot pain. And unfortunately, if I wasn't home, the diet was disregarded. After a while, since a single type of insulin was not enough, they had him to start a second one. One type was the regular immediate-release type, the other one was extended-release type. It was our daughter Zeynep who was helping him and making a game out of it. When it was time for an insulin injection, Zeynep would come running, "I'll do the needle, daddy!" My husband would insert the needle, and my daughter would inject the medicine.

Gokhan was taking insulin injections twice a day, as well as using anxiety medication. He had not stopped taking the medications he started while he was in the military, even though he was supposed to do so. He said that the anxiety medication made him feel safe and well.

Unfortunately, when he was later arrested and he needed them the most, he would not be allowed to take those medications, and his diabetes and panic attacks would reach their peak. During the daytime he was getting tortured and in the nighttime he was severely suffering from hallucinations and nightmares. During those days that he spent in a cell under custody, he often said to his friends, "I can't breathe! I am suffocating! I am dying!"

WHO DIED OF TORTURE?

Well, it all started with the "17/25 Corruption Operations[10]" in December 2013. On that day, of course, no one could foresee what a dictator could do to avoid being trialed in a court for the corruption, bribery, and all sorts of other unlawful acts that he has committed. No one could foresee how many innocent people would die because of the ambitions of that dictator. A few days after the corruption scandal got public, the police chief and policemen who were conducting the corruption operations were arrested and imprisoned. Moreover, the issue soon shifted from the legal ground to an element of political hatred.

We weren't impacted by the events of that period.

---

10 The December 17-25, 2013, corruption scandal in Turkey refers to a criminal investigation that involves several key people in the Turkish government. Prosecutors accused 14 people, including several family members of the cabinet ministers, the director of state-owned bank (Halkbank) and Turkish-Iranian businessman Reza Zarrab, of bribery, corruption, fraud, money laundering and gold smuggling. In March 2016, Reza Zarrab was arrested in Miami. In November 2017, Zarrab cooperated with federal prosecutors and has become key witness in the case of money laundering and violating sanctions on Iran.

Gokhan, however, was very upset about the atrocities suffered by the police officers who were imprisoned. He was getting so sad, when he used to hear news about those police officers in jail, such as: "The heating in their wards was turned on during the hot summer days and turned off in the cold winter days... Water was often cut off for no reason... In the month of Ramadan[11], they were not provided any food during the time of breaking the fast... Prison guards eating and drinking in front of the inmates while the inmates were fasting." All sorts of physical and mental tortures were being committed in violation of the rules of international law.

    Gokhan could not turn a blind eye to all of these and he was criticizing the politicians at every turn. Sometimes he was getting engaged in long and heated discussions with people around him. He just couldn't put up with all the lies and slanders against the Hizmet movement. Me, on the other hand, I wasn't a person who liked to speak her mind or argue with other people. In fact, in the school that I was working, people supporting the AKP and other political parties were keeping a distance from each other and I was the only one who was in good terms with both groups. I believed that political differences and

---

11 Ramadan is the ninth month of the Islamic calendar, observed by Muslims worldwide as a month of fasting, prayer, reflection and community.

worldviews should not distance us.

Gokhan was most upset when we went to Konya during the 2015 summer. My relatives were not involved with the Hizmet Movement. Naturally, some believed in the fabricated lies they have been reading in the media and made very serious accusations against Gokhan and the Hizmet Movement. As Gokhan tried to explain the atrocities and slander against the innocent people, he found recklessness and insults in return, which seriously injured him. He burst into tears once and told me, "Let's pack our bags and let's get out of here! I feel like they're swearing at my mother, I can't take this anymore!" I convinced him to stay, saying, "We just got here, my parents will be very upset, let's stay a little longer." After that visit, he didn't want to go to Konya anymore. He retreated into his shell, day by day.

Of course, I was suffering a lot from this situation that we were dragged into. But I also knew that it was useless to argue with people who didn't want to see or to hear. I was able to clearly observe the people mentioned in the chapter Araf in Quran: *"They have hearts but they won't understand. They have eyes but they won't see. They have ears but they won't hear."* For so many years I had been reading in the books about the events that will occur before the end of time, such as Dajjal (AntiChrist), about how he would deceive masses of people and how people would follow him like herds. Alas! I was witnessing a very similar time period now!

When we returned to Istanbul from Konya that summer, we were able to breathe a little. It had felt like a lot of dirt thrown at us, and we couldn't clean it up. We couldn't tell anyone that we were innocent because everyone was hypnotized by the media. And because we were so upset, we chose not to talk to anyone about these issues. We were just coming together with our close friends in Hizmet. Well, when we were coming together with them, of course we were talking about God and about doing good, not about "how to perform a coup!", as they would later slander us. We were reading the Qur'an, Risale-i Nur[12] books, and focusing on our inner development and peace.

To tell the truth, Gokhan and I had never talked along the topics like "What is going on with the country?" or "What about us? What if this persecution finds us one

---

[12] Collection of the books written by Said Nursi. Rather than being a Quranic commentary which expounds all its verses giving the immediate reasons for their revelation and the apparent meanings of the words and sentences, the Risale-i Nur is a commentary which expounds the meaning of the Quranic truths. The verses mostly expounded in the Risale-i Nur are those concerned with the truths of belief, such as the divine names and attributes and the divine activity in the universe, the divine existence and unity, resurrection, Prophethood, divine determining or destiny, and man's duties of worship.

day?" After all, we had not committed a single crime in our lives, we were ordinary people living our lives. What could happen anyhow? Later, I was going to find out about a conversation Gokhan had with his friends. When one of his friends expressed his concerns saying "What if they arrest us, too?" my husband joked, "Oh come on. Nobody dies of torture! Anyway, if they take me in, I will give them your names, so that we can continue our friendship in Silivri prison!" They all laughed that day, without knowing about the dark clouds approaching over the entire country.

Chapter 4

Country roads, take me home...

to the place I belong!

The Life and Legacy of Gokhan Acikkollu

WASH ME IN THE RAIN OF MY VILLAGE

Gokhan had always wanted to be a martyr. One of his friends told him one day, "According to some religious narrations, If the diabetics don't complain about their disease and don't rebel against God, they would be considered as martyrs, even if they die in their beds." Upon hearing that, Gokhan stood up and raised his hands, praying: "Oh, I wish to be one of them! I really wish!"

When we used to go to my small village in Konya, especially if it was drizzling, he would keep singing the song, "Let them wash me in the rain of my village…" The cemetery was so close to our house, he'd point his finger at it and say, "Right there, bury me right there." I'd get so upset and say, "Don't talk like this! Be careful what you wish for, you just might get it!"

I told you before, July 15th is my son Fatih's birthday. Until 2016, for seventeen years, we celebrated that day happily with a birthday cake. It was July 15 again, our cake was ready, and as a gift we got him a t-shirt from a brand that he'd wanted for a long time. Well, it was not a big party or anything like that, we were just going to celebrate within the family. We were just enjoying our son's birthday cake when we began hearing loud voices outside. We turned on the TV, the Bosphorus Bridge was blockaded by soldiers, and the public TV station anchorwoman was reading the announcement of a military coup. We were absolutely shocked! And when we began hearing gun sounds outside, we got extremely nervous.

Gokhan was a historian who knew the history of coups very well. Surprised, he said: "It's Friday and rush hour, traffic is terrible, it's weird to start the coup at this time of the day and by blocking bridges". Soon after, the president of Turkey went live on television and directly blamed the Hizmet movement for the coup, called people to go out to the streets and protect their country. We were all confused and thought, "What the hell is going on here?" We couldn't even think of the possibility that this could eventually affect our family.

We stayed home all day long on Saturday and followed the events, but Sunday was my brother-in-law's wedding. We had to drive from Umraniye to the European side of the city, crossing the Bosphorus Bridge. The day before, the bridge was completely washed with the street washing trucks. Who knows how many young soldiers were slaughtered there that night? How many people were murdered there that night regardless of whether they were guilty of anything or not? Lynched and executed without trial! It was really strange that the local government had immediately washed the bridge and everything on it, all the crime evidence was washed away and lost.

After the wedding ceremony on Sunday, we had dinner with a large family group at a restaurant, as previously planned. I'll never forget the waiter looking at us and grumbling, "There's been a coup in the country, and they're having a wedding."

"FORGIVE ME"

On that ominous night, before even anyone realized what was going on, the president of the country had already targeted us and signaled who would be the real victims of that night. But we still didn't think of the possibility that they would eventually harm us. We did not know yet how much the judiciary had fallen prey to the ruling party, of course. If we were charged with a crime, either personally or as part of the Hizmet movement, they should have brought forth some kind of evidence of a crime, of course. We wouldn't be convicted of a crime that we had not committed. There was rule of law in the country, after all. In retrospect, after everything we have witnessed in the last 6 years since that coup plot, how incredibly naive we were then!

We were supposed to go to our hometown on Monday morning, July 18th. It was not a decision we

Country roads, take me home…to the place I belong!

made because of the current situation; we had planned it so many days ago. We jumped into our car and left for Buyukoz village in the Ahirli district of Konya. We just wanted to get away from the Istanbul's dark agenda and take a breather. We didn't get into any argument with my family members or anyone else in the village. They didn't bring it up either, and we had a nice time together. That was good for us.

My brother-in-law would have another wedding ceremony and henna night in the city of Hatay a few days later. On the way there, we learned that a friend of Gokhan was taken into custody. They had arrested him in his hometown where he was spending his vacation with his family together. I was incredibly upset, I stopped the car several times and got out so I could breathe and calm down. I was asking questions to Gokhan to get some details but also trying not to scare the children in the car. It had not been even a week since the coup attempt; it was not even clear who attempted it. What kind of evidence could they have had to arrest a person who had an ordinary job?

Apparently, someone else who was taken into custody had snitched on Gokhan's friend to police. When I first heard that, I couldn't accept it: "How can someone do that?" Gokhan answered: "They broke his arm, tortured him severely. He had to give them names." It was still beyond my grasp and said: "But he could have thought that they would torture his friend even more. How could he commit such a betrayal?" Gokhan was upset, but he didn't react as I did. "You never know what people are going through in prison," he said.

We arrived in Hatay in this mood and didn't have any fun at the henna night of course. At some point in the evening, I overheard someone saying "At last, the state of emergency has been declared, let's find out all the traitors!" His words against the Hizmet movement made me shudder. Not because I was guilty of anything, but because I could see how this persecution would harm innocent people instead of the real culprits.

At some point, Gokhan was chatting with a friend who owned a farm in Hatay, and I joined them. My husband jokingly said, "They might fire us from our jobs soon. Perhaps you can give us a job in your farm here." His friend smiled and said, "Anything for a hard-working man like you, it will be my pleasure". We all laughed together.

Later that night we returned from Hatay and being so tired, we immediately went to sleep. The next day we woke up to the news that my children's schools were

Country roads, take me home...to the place I belong!

shut down permanently by a government decree. Yusuf Tekin, the undersecretary of the Ministry of National Education, was talking on the TV station CNN Turk. There was still no organizational scheme of the coup nor any concrete knowledge about who was behind it. But over 1,000 schools which are affiliated with the Hizmet movement were immediately shut down, and 21,000 of the 27,000 teachers in those schools had their work permits and licenses revoked. All of the 138,000 students in those schools had to enroll in other schools.[13] Two of those students were my children.

Gokhan immediately bought a high-speed train ticket for the next day back to Istanbul. He suggested going back together, but I wanted to stay with my family for a few more days and clear my mind. In Istanbul, he would try to transfer our children to a different school and

---

13 Turkish Criminal Law, Article 76: **(1)** Execution of any one of the following acts under a plan against members of national, racial or religious groups with the intention of destroying the complete or part of the group, creates the legal consequence of an offense defined as genocide.
a) Voluntary manslaughter
b) To act with the intention of giving severe corporal or spiritual injury,
c) To impose conditions that make survival of complete or part of the group members impossible,
d) To impose that prevent births in the group,
e) To transfer minors of a group to another group,
(2) A person who commits the offense of genocide is sentenced to heavy imprisonment.

also find a way to help the family of his friend who was arrested a few days ago.

Friday, July 22, 2016. I dropped Gokhan off at the train station around 7:00 a.m. We had paid the children's school tuition fees in advance to take advantage of the early enrollment opportunity. I said, "Take care of yourself. If you can get the money back, that is fine... otherwise, it's not a big deal." Of course, that wasn't our main problem at the time, but as it turned out, our government (!) would illegally seize that money which tens of thousands of parents like us worked very hard to make.

Gokhan showed his ticket at the gate and then turned around and looked at me. It was weird because I could not stop looking at him either. I will never forget that moment, he was wearing light brown pants, a light pink shirt, a navy blue linen jacket, and his black shoes. I still remember how at that moment I shuddered to my bones! Why? I don't know. The phrase "*Hakkini helal et!*"[14] spilled from my lips. He whispered, nodding, "You, too." And then he was gone. Of course, we didn't know it at the time, but this would be the last time we'd see each other in this world.

---

14 A phrase in Turkish, meaning "Please forgive me for all my faults towards you with or without knowing. Let's please make a peace between our hearts and let's keep that peace!".

Country roads, take me home…to the place I belong!

"I DOUBT MYSELF; I NEVER DOUBT HIM!"

My cousin was living in downtown Konya. The day before Gokhan was leaving to Istanbul, we had come to their place. After we left Gokhan at the train station in the morning, we had a breakfast together with my cousin, children and parents. On the way back to the village, Gokhan called. He had just arrived in Istanbul, and he sounded worried. "My school principal just called; I'm suspended!" he said. I was shocked! I tried to comfort him but he was very nervous and said: "Even the medication I use costs a lot of money. How are we going to survive?" I still tried to give him hope and said: "Don't worry, everything will be alright. I still have my job. Besides, it is God Who will provide for us. Please don't be sad!"

Even though I did not say so to Gokhan, I was quite demoralized myself. As a matter of fact, soon after Gokhan's call, my school principal called and said: "You have been suspended…You have to come and sign the termination papers!" I asked him why I was suspended, but he didn't say anything. I said that I couldn't come and asked him to e-mail me the papers. He said, "You'd better come here. I have to serve the papers in person!" I asked him over and over again what was written on the paperwork, but he didn't want to say. Instead, he just passed it off saying "The possibility of being a member of FETO[15], being a member of the labor union; giving support to FETO financially or through social media." He was just mumbling. I was not a member of any labor union, because I never believed in them anyhow. I did not have any Twitter, Instagram, or Facebook accounts, either. Besides, since when are these considered as crime anyhow?[16]

I had served my country for 23 years, paid my taxes, never committed any crime, tried to be a good citizen and a good person. In return, today, I was suspended from my job without any reasonable justification. And I was going to be dismissed permanently with a second decree law on October 29, 2016, without even being allowed to defend myself against their slanders. I was very upset, but God bless my family, they have always supported me. "Don't worry about a thing!" my late father said. "I can take care of you and your family. You can always move to our place!"

---

15 FETO is the name used by the current Erdogan government to describe the Hizmet movement. The Hizmet movement is based on moral values and advocacy of universal access to education, civil society, tolerance and peace
16 Turkish Criminal Law, Article 21: (1) In order to consider an act as an offense, a crime has to be intended by the offender. Malice is an intention to cause harm being aware of the legal consequences of the crime defined in the laws.

Country roads, take me home…to the place I belong!

In my 23 years of career, I had no negative marks on my personal record. On the contrary, I had often received awards and compliments from my superiors. Then all of a sudden, I was declared a terrorist and dismissed from my job. About two years later, when I was painting a window frame in a European country where I was living as a refugee, I would think of that day on which I was dismissed. I took a picture of the window frames that I was painting and shared it in my WhatsApp status with a message: *"I studied for 17 years, worked for 23 years. Now I'm painting window frames at the peak of my career."*

Later on that day I called Gokhan to tell him I was also suspended. We talked briefly, and the next morning I got a call from him when he was waiting outside Zeynep's school. The school building was surrounded by police, and they wouldn't let anyone in claiming that "school inventory was being counted." So, he neither could get the reimbursements of the children's tuition fees, nor could he transfer the children to another school. That phone conversation was the last time I had ever talked to him!

Apparently, he called a friend afterward and said, "I'm so overwhelmed, can we meet?" Of course, I was going to find out about this much later. They went to a soup kitchen together that afternoon. The news channel "*A Haber*" was on TV. My husband got even more disturbed and upset when he saw on TV the defamatory news and slanders targeting the Hizmet movement. The anchorman was lying about the murders which couldn't (!) be solved for decades and how the culprits of those murders were actually related to the Hizmet movement! Gokhan asked them to turn off the TV a few times, but when they just ignored him he had a nervous breakdown. His friend picked him up quickly and took him somewhere else to avoid any quarrel.

One of the reasons Gokhan went to Istanbul was to help the family of his detained friend. Unfortunately, he wouldn't have had a chance to do that. The day he had arrived in Istanbul, another friend had called him and warned him against visiting his detained friend or his family, saying: "You might get in trouble if he gives your name", and he added: "Don't stay at your own home for a while if you can." Gokhan didn't listen to his advice. He was thinking that all this was a big mistake and sooner or later everyone would come back to their senses. Gokhan, on that phone conversation, had told his friend: "I trust my detained friend more than I trust myself." Unfortunately, only one day later, he would see that he was wrong!

Country roads, take me home…to the place I belong!

"IF THEY HAD THE CHANCE, THEY'D KILL YOU TOO!"

We never got on the phone with Gokhan again after that morning on Saturday, July 23rd. He came home and went to bed early probably due to stress and grief. How do I know that? From the statements of the housing complex manager, who was asked to be present as a witness by the police during the search of our house. She said, "When the police officers entered into the house, the lights were off." I was going to learn all of what happened that night from the statements of that lady, who got frightened later and refused to testify what she had witnessed that night.

Apparently, around 10:30 p.m. that night, the housing complex manager had noticed many civilians walking inside the complex. When she went near them and asked who they were, they said that they are police. When she said, "Well, how can I help you?" she was told, "If we need you, we will call you; you can go home for now."

As a matter of fact, about half an hour later, the police called her and asked her to come to the apartment A-27 to be present as a witness. Upon hearing that, she called the complex security to know who is staying in A-27. Well, it was our apartment. When she asked what kind of people we are, they responded "Just a couple of teachers, no problems whatsoever, ordinary people, respectful, always paying their management fees on time." I am just citing the rest as the housing manager lady told me:

> "Mr. Acikkollu opened the door and the police told him that there was a detention order against him. Shocked, he asked, 'What's the matter? What am I accused of? Do I need to call my lawyer?" He was told that it was not necessary for now. In a typical police search, the police turns on a video camera, and they enter every room together with someone who is living in that property. But they had not turned the video camera on, and what is more, suddenly the police threw him to the ground face down and handcuffed him behind his back. Meanwhile, they were beating him and yelling at him: "Are you a member of FETO? Are you involved in the coup? Do you know people such and such?"[17]

Why did around 30 police officers come to arrest an ordinary teacher? Why were they carrying assault rifles in their hands? Why did they have snow masks on their faces? Why would they start torturing him at home for

---

[17] Turkish Criminal Law, Article 77: **(1)** Execution of any one of the following acts systematically under a plan against a sector of a community for political, philosophical, racial or religious reasons, creates the legal consequence of an offense against humanity.
a) Voluntary manslaughter
b) To act with the intention of giving injury to another person
c) Torturing, infliction of severe suffering, or forcing a person to live as a slave
d) To restrict freedom

Country roads, take me home…to the place I belong!

answers they would easily get if they had only asked normally? Why this unlawful persecution?

Everything was developing so fast and so unusual, the police was brutally beating Gokhan, meanwhile turning our house into a mess. They literally left nothing unturned, shoes in the shoe rack, clothes in the wardrobe, children's books, pots and pans in kitchen cabinets, even the flower pots on the balcony were scattered on the floor, and the house was turned into a war zone. What did they think? What were they hoping to find? In which Hizmet member's house did they find anything other than books? These questions remain unanswered even six years after the incident.

Most terrifyingly, a man who was lying down on the ground and on his face, who was handcuffed behind his back was beaten brutally while being questioned. Before long, Gokhan, whose panic attack was triggered and his blood sugar skyrocketed, entered in a diabetic coma. One of the police officers brought sugar cubes from the kitchen and tried to stuff them in Gokhan's mouth. Thankfully, the complex manager who was witnessing the entire thing intervened and convinced the police for the insulin injection using the syringe they found in Gokhan's briefcase. They, of course, haven't removed his handcuffs meanwhile.

Unfortunately, what I know about that night is limited to what the manager lady told me. But I don't think she told me everything she witnessed. Since at some point in time on that evening she told to police that she can't stand it anymore and she wants to leave. Who knows what kind of torture she witnessed? The police did not let her go, saying, "You're a witness, you have to stay until we are done!" The manager lady insisted, "I don't want to see all this. Bring him with you and do whatever you're going to do at the police station! Besides, I am Alevi[18], I have nothing to do with any of this!" In return, the response she got was very interesting: "If these people had a chance, they would kill you Alewis. You see, just a week ago, the soldiers these people trained had fired bullets at people!"

But my Lord is my witness that we had nothing to do with anything that had happened during that coup night of one week ago. We were ordinary people sitting at home, unaware of anything...let alone firing bullets or giving orders to those who fired bullets.

When that lady wasn't allowed to leave the house that evening, she decided to go into some other room and wait

---

18 Around 10-15% of the population living in Turkey is Alawis, who are following a belief system that incorporates aspects of Shi'a and Sunni Islam as well as the traditions of other and much older belief systems in the region.

Country roads, take me home…to the place I belong!

there, since she really couldn't stand it anymore.

Those who had slandered people like us would not be able to find a single weapon in any house they have searched in the last six years since that coup plot…not in our house, nor in any other Hizmet-affiliated person's house, car, or any property. Not a single weapon! They only found books! We were nobody but peaceful guards of Love! Hundreds of thousands of people would be arrested on terrorism charges on the grounds of the books they had at their homes.[19] Gokhan was one of those people who got arrested in such an inhumane way without any evidence whatsoever.

I would also like to mention a tragicomic incident regarding the police search of our house. The officers who turned our house into a mess during that so-called search looked also inside my dower chest and found an image of Tweety - yes, that yellow canary in the animated

---

19 Turkish Criminal Law, Article 7: **(1)** A person may neither be punished nor subject to a security measure for an act which does not constitute an offense according to the law in force at the time of commission of the offense. Also, one may neither be punished nor subject to a security measure for an act which does not constitute an offense according to the law which is put into force after the commission of the offense. Where a punishment or security precautions of that sort is imposed, its execution and legal consequences are spontaneously abrogated.

(2) Where there are differences between provisions of the law in force at the time of commission of the offense and the provisions of the law subsequently put into force, the law which is in favor of the perpetrator is applied and enforced.

cartoon – which was clumsily drawn on a piece of paper. They asked Gokhan, "What's this? Tell us right now what kind of a secret code this is?" They had beaten him another round just for that. How could my dear Gokhan know that when our son was a baby, I had knitted for him a sweater with a Tweety motif and in order not to forget about it, I had drawn the pattern on a sheet of paper and put it in the chest? Even I had forgotten about it. The arguments they used to declare us terrorists were as funny and ridiculous as that cartoon character. On that evening, he looked at the paper shown to him and said with fearful eyes, "I don't know anything about this, it probably belongs to my wife or to my son!" One of the policemen then roared, waving this ultra-important Tweety-bird terror evidence in his hand that he just found: "Find his wife right now! Arrest her, too!"

Did Gokhan suffer a lot of pain that evening? While he was beaten and humiliated, did he ever think of us? Did he get scared that I'd be taken into custody, too? Did he foresee that the officers who swarmed our house that night would eventually murder him? I don't know, but again, according to the housing complex manager, he kept asking desperately, "Why are you doing this? My brother's a police officer, too. And I am a person who loves his country and nation!" Alas! The enforcement

Country roads, take me home...to the place I belong!

of law had become so corrupt in the entire country that it was the police who would decide who was guilty and who should be arrested, and not according to concrete evidence but according to their personal feelings. Upon hearing what Gokhan said, one of them shouted: "Arrest his brother, too!"

What happened then? After a couple of hours of house search and torturous interrogation, Gokhan was dragged out of the house without even being allowed to change his clothes and take his medication. Humiliating him even further in front of the people in the neighborhood, he was thrown into a police car while still being beaten, totally violating the universal law which states that "everyone is innocent until proven guilty." According to the manager lady as they were taking Gokhan away in the car, they were still beating him.[20]

---

[20] Turkish Criminal Law, Article 109: Deprivation of Liberty

(1) Any person who unlawfully restricts the freedom of a person by preventing him from traveling or living in a place is sentenced to imprisonment from one year to five years.

(2) If a person uses physical power or threat or deception to perform an act or during commission of offense, then he is sentenced to imprisonment from two years to seven years.

(3) In case of commission of this offense;
a) By use of a weapon,
b) Jointly by a group of persons,
c) By virtue of a public office,
d) By undue influence based on public office,
e) Against antecedents, descendents or spouse,
f) Against a child or a person who cannot protect himself due to corporal

Laptops, cell phones, passports, cameras, a flash drive which actually my daughter was using for her school assignments, even a photograph taken during one of my friend's engagement ceremony were all taken away from our house that night.

Can you imagine what Gokhan lived through inside the police station behind the closed doors? The police had not even hesitated to beat and torture him publicly that night during his arrest? Imagine what that manager lady could have witnessed during those hours in our house that caused her to seek psychological support afterward! We have brought all the evidence of physical and psychological torture to the court after Gokhan's death. But all our accusations have been repeatedly denied by the legal authorities.

When my husband was tortured to death, I had nothing left to lose anymore. I knew that they would be held accountable in the Hereafter, but I wanted them to

---

or spiritual disability, the punishment imposed according to the above subsections is increased by one fold.

(4) If this offense results with gross economical loss of the victim, the offender additionally is imposed a punitive fine up to one thousand days.

(5) In case of commission of offense with sexual intent, the punishments to be imposed according to above subsections are increased by one half.

(6) The provisions relating to felonious injury are additionally applied in case of commission of aggravated form of this offense which creates the consequences of felonious injury.

be brought to trial in this world, too. So I started...digging a well with a needle. I had requested our housing complex manager lady to put everything that she had seen on that night in writing. I thought that her testimony would change the course of our case. To my astonishment, she denied everything that she had witnessed and said: "I'm on the side of my government, there's no torture or anything like that! Don't get me involved!" She also refused to provide the security camera footage of that evening. It was my legal right to ask for that footage. But her only response was: "Just don't involve me in this, OK!?" I expressed my resentment saying "You were Alevi, weren't you? And I've been telling my students for years that you are honest people. How dos this suit your belief system?" Ironically, I have remembered that some time ago that same lady posted on her WhatsApp status a post which read "Don't get deceived by the perfumes that people use. One should smell trustworthy". I reminded her of that post and said, "How do you think you smell to me right now?"

"YOUR HUSBAND HAS BEEN TAKEN INTO CUSTODY!"

I've thought about it a lot later on. I was at my parents' house in Konya when they brutally beat Gokhan and took him away in a police car only to continue their torture[21] all night long. I don't know whether it had something to do with a kind of premonition, but I remember it was a pretty gloomy night for me, too. I woke up from my sleep many times for no reason and ran next to the window to get some fresh air. It was the first time I'd ever been through something like this, and I was trying to calm myself down by reciting prayers. I remember thinking, "What is this chest pain and racing heartbeat all about? I hope police doesn't show up to our house tonight!"

At 7:00 a.m. on Sunday morning, when an unknown number called me from the European side of Istanbul, I jumped out of my sleep. It was a stone-cold voice: "I'm from the counter-terrorism branch…calling to inform you that your husband has been detained!" A chill ran down my spine! "What? Why? How?" I was asking questions one after another. "I can't give you any further information," he said. I tried one more time desperately "But why!?" Same answer: "We can't tell you!" When I said: "Where are you located? Where should I come to see my husband?", the phone got hung up all of a sudden!

What a terrible thing it is to have to deal with

---

21 Turkish Criminal Law, Article 94: **(1)** Any public officer who causes severe bodily or mental pain, or loss of consciousness or ability to act, or dishonors a person, is sentenced to imprisonment from three years to twelve years.

Country roads, take me home...to the place I belong!

uncertainty! That's when I felt it in my bones. What happened? Why did they take him into custody? Where did they take him, is he safe and sound? I didn't know anything! I woke up my parents and said in panic: "They arrested Gokhan. I have to go back to Istanbul immediately!"

There's something else I have to say about that morning: I told you earlier my brother-in-law was a police officer. As soon as I calmed down a little, I called him and said, "They've taken your brother into custody. Can you please go to the *Vatan* police department? Maybe he is there. If he sees you, he would feel a bit better. You don't even need to say to anyone that he is your brother." The response I received from him felt like a slap in the face: "Please leave me out of this!" Go figure! He was Gokhan's brother from the same mother and father! Well, I heard his message loud and clear, from that moment on I had never involved him in anything. Whenever I needed something, I've asked my own family for help.

I just couldn't wait, I had to go to Istanbul as soon as possible and find Gokhan. But my parents didn't want me to drive 800 kilometers all the way to Istanbul given the situation I was in. So they called my brother from Istanbul and he arrived to Konya with the first bus that he found. As soon as my brother arrived and rested for a few hours, we left together.

My parents and I separated in tears for the first time. They had full confidence in me of course, but at that moment I felt the need to explain myself and said, crying, "We have nothing to do with the coup, nothing! Everything will come to light eventually." They prayed in tears and sent their children into the unknown.

My brother had already made an 8-hour-long bus ride and he was now driving the car after only a few hours of rest. We were both so tired, mentally and physically, that we had no energy to talk to each other. Perhaps for the first time, our return from Konya to Istanbul was so quiet and sorrowful. My children, in fear, were trying to understand what was going on and had probably questions like "What does arrest mean? What happens when you're arrested? Where is our father?" My daughter was only seven years old and she didn't understand much. My son was aware of everything but he was, like always, suppressing his feelings. Neither of them asked me anything along the way.

We drove all night long. Around sunrise in the morning, he couldn't stay awake anymore and he fell asleep while driving! The car departed its lane and came in contact with the crash barriers on the side of the road.

Country roads, take me home…to the place I belong!

The sound woke him up immediately so he straightened the car. We could have had a major car accident, God protected us.

On the road to Istanbul, I was thinking "What is the worst that could happen? We haven't committed any crime, what are they going to accuse us of?" Our innocence was giving me some kind of confidence. But then I remembered all those news and pictures they were showing on TV channels about how they were torturing so many innocent people and I really got worried about Gokhan. I had a lot of thoughts spinning in my head along the road, but my Lord knows I had never thought of the possibility that he would be killed. I was just thinking about whether he would be released after they take his statement or not.

WE ARE NOT TERRORISTS, BUT YOU ARE THIEVES!

We arrived in Istanbul early Monday morning. We didn't run into anyone when we entered the house, so I didn't see any reaction from people living in the neighborhood. Actually, I was not in a state of mind to notice anything around. But in the following days, those who had previously called me almost every day, especially the parents of students with whom we shared the same housing complex, would not even stop by to say a quick hello. Well, did I care? Not at all! I just wanted this nightmare to end as soon as possible.

I stepped into our house which looked like a total wreck. Even though I was a working mother of two children, I was always keeping our house super clean and tidy. And now, everything was in a total mess, the carpets were full of dirt and mud stains, cigarette butts were all over the place. I guess they had intentionally turned our house into a disaster zone to add extra stress and sadness to our situation. Did I get upset to see my house like that? God knows I was not. I don't care about worldly possessions. It was just I had neither mental nor physical strength to clean the house at that moment.

I didn't mind it myself, but I wish my children had not seen their house like that. When I saw how scared and disturbed they were, I immediately began to clean up the house. While cleaning, I was grumbling meanwhile, "What kind of police are you? Is this the way to search a house? Mud stains everywhere! Cigarette butts? Give me a break! People live here!"

Fortunately, my children went to clean their rooms and did not see how shattered I was. Whenever I lifted something from the floor, the related scene enacted in my mind, and I got totally devastated. Two years ago, Gokhan had given me a monolith ring as a birthday present. I found its box, empty. I looked everywhere for the ring, in vain. The police had pretty much stolen an expensive ring in a house that they had searched to find an evidence of crime! I got very upset about it not because of its financial value, but because it was a gift from my husband. Well, it was not the only thing which was missing. All the computers, cell phones, hard drives, flash drives, and cameras were gone, under the pretense of investigation.

I don't normally feel upset for financial losses. I just say, "Let it be a charity from me." But I got so upset about that ring and those electronic devices they brought with them. After Gokhan's death, our lawyer and I repeatedly filed petitions to take them back, but our efforts have been futile. All our family memories were on those devices. My daughter's first Quran reading ceremony...our children's birthday parties...a funny song that my husband performed for our daughter...our past, our future. On that evening, they had not only stolen my husband but also our family, our memories, and the witnesses of those memories.

While I was cleaning up the house, my mind was

constantly on Gokhan. Every five minutes I was using my phone to look for a lawyer on the internet. I had also recorded the number of the police office which had called to let me know that Gokhan was detained. I called them several times to find out where they had taken Gokhan. But I couldn't learn anything.

FOR GOD'S SAKE, SOMEONE TELL ME WHERE MY HUSBAND IS!

We had arrived in Istanbul on Monday morning. I cleaned up the mess in the house, looked for a lawyer, and tried to find out where my husband was. In the evening we went to my brother's house on the European side. We were going to stay there for a while.

The only thing I had in my hand was a phone number. It belonged to the police office that informed me that my husband had been detained on the previous day. I called that number several times. "Please" I said, "my husband has panic attacks and diabetes. You didn't even let him take his medication when he left the house. Please tell me where he is located, and I'll bring his medication!" They were not telling me anything. I called them three or four times every day. I kept saying, "My husband is sick" and they kept saying, "There are doctors here, they're taking care of him. He's fine!" and they were hanging up the phone. Those people who were answering my phone were not even interested in who I was or what my husband's name was. None of them asked even once: "What is your husband's name?" I finally stormed at them: "How do you know he's doing fine? You haven't even asked me his name yet!" They hung up the phone right away!

I felt so helpless! I was calling many times every day, patiently explaining my situation to every different person who answered the phone. "Where's my husband?" No answer! "Look, I want to hire a lawyer, but I need some information." They said, "You can't!" When I asked "But is a person not allowed to have his lawyer present when he is being questioned?", they replied: "If the prosecutor's office thinks it is necessary, a lawyer will be appointed by the court." Upon hearing that, I said "But how am I supposed to know whether my husband is provided a lawyer by the court or not? I don't even know where he is kept." They said I could call the Istanbul Bar Association, and maybe they would be of some help.

When I was dealing with all these things, I had no idea where they were keeping Gokhan, whether he was safe and sound, and how his health was. I didn't know anything. I would find out much later that they had taken him from home around 1 a.m. on July 24th. It was around

8 am in the morning when they brought him to a cell in the building of Vatan Police Department. Where was he held for all those seven hours? In a room with no cameras, no law, no mercy, and no humanity! A torture room! His cellmates would later tell that when Gokhan was brought and they had seen him for the first time around 8 am, he was severely in pain and holding his ribs.

Whenever I think about it, I feel like I am losing my mind. When we were driving from Konya to Istanbul, trying to hide my tears from my children and constantly praying for him, they were ruthlessly kicking Gokhan in his face, back, and legs. When I was trying to clean up the mess that the police had left in our house, he was in a diabetic coma. At that night, when I was exhausted and fell asleep, Gokhan was taken from his cell to get tortured. Even if he was allowed to sleep that day for some time, he was living the same tortures over and over again in his nightmares, because his panic attacks were playing tricks on him.

I kept doing the only thing that I could. I called that number every day, begging the officer whoever was answering that phone that day. Days were passing by. I finally lost my patience and screamed my lungs out: "For God's sake, at least tell me where he is. He needs to take his medication!" That made the officer very angry. "What the hell are you screaming about? And don't bring God into this!" he roared. "There is no further information. There are doctors here, they're taking care of him, and he is fine. Don't call here anymore!" Then he hung up on me again.

The next day, I just couldn't afford not to call again. Thank God, the person on the phone had some mercy in his heart this time. When I explained the situation, he said, "Bring his medicine and clothes, and we'll deliver them to him." It was the first time someone had actually listened to me and responded. When I told him I didn't know where my husband was, he asked for my husband's name and last name, and after a short amount of time, he said "Come to the *Vatan* Police Department." God bless that police officer! He pulled me out of the dark hole I had been in for days.

I was so excited. My brother and I rushed to our house in Umraniye and prepared a small bag for Gokhan. When I remember this now, a bitter smile passes over my lips because I had even put personal care items in that bag, thinking that the standard legal process would run as it should regarding the custody procedure. Two pairs of casual clothes, slippers, underwear, soap, toothbrush and toothpaste. He was being tortured every day, he couldn't even get any decent food or water, and here I was, putting in the bag a toothbrush! It's tragicomic when you think about it! I also made sure to put his medication in the bag. In a hurry, I placed a note into one of his medication bottles: "*We love you very much. Don't worry about us. Take care of yourself. May God protect you! Your family.*"

Actually, there was another reason why I wrote this note. I had heard from some of my friends that the police was threatening some of the detainees by saying "We have arrested your wife, too". And they were forcing them to provide information and names. I knew that while they were searching our house they had told him "We're going to take your wife into custody!" because of the Tweety figure they found in the dower chest. So I just wanted him to know that we were doing fine.

On the evening of July 27th, I went to the *Vatan* Police Department with my son and brother. But on the way, my brother said, "What if they arrest you too? You better wait outside!" My son and brother went in, I stayed out. The custody rooms were on the 7. floor under the ground.

In the meantime, I was outside watching the people around. During those days, in the entire country so-called "democracy rallies" were held. People were spending the entire day and night on streets with flags in their hands. It

Country roads, take me home...to the place I belong!

was so crowded and such a chaos was prevailing around... it felt like an apocalypse. Live-streaming TV vans were everywhere, the *"Dombra"* propaganda song of the AKP[22] was echoing in the entire city. People were protecting (!) the country with flags in their hands. I could hear a man with a microphone in his hand shouting, "We're going to fight with them! Traitors! Terrorists!" I felt very bad at that moment. Were they talking about us? Although they had not seen anything wrong with us? Gokhan, me, our brothers and sisters in Hizmet... Were we really such evil, vicious people?

I looked at the men and women who lay down on the grass field across the Vatan Street, most of the women wearing headscarves...eating sunflower seeds and nuts, enjoying a cup of tea in their hands, having a late picnic...waving flags here and there, protecting (!) their government and their country, listening to the man with microphone, who talks nonsensical hypocrisy. Thousands and thousands of rude, arrogant, and ignorant people, who were absolutely convinced that they were the only true patriots in the country, shouting "Traitooooors! Terroriiiiists!" while lying on the grass. I don't think I can

---

[22] Abbreviation of the *Adalet ve Kalkinma Partisi* in Turkish, Justice and Development Party, which is ruling Turkey since 2002 under Recep Tayyip Erdogan.

ever forget that sight.

I just couldn't take all this anymore. For so many days, I was dealing with extreme stress and grief, and trying to hide it from my children. But I just couldn't help it anymore, and began crying loudly. I was crying my heart out. Right then, a man in pretty shabby clothes came towards me - I would later learn that he was an undercover police officer. Handing me a small bottle of water, he asked, "Ma'am, are you all right? Is your husband in custody or something?" I could barely nod my head as I took a few sips of water. "Is he a soldier or police officer?" he asked. Crying, I screamed: "Teacher! He is a teacher! For God's sake, what does a teacher have to do with a military coup!?" "Don't worry," he comforted me, "Probably he will be released in a few days. Besides, look around you. It is such a mess everywhere. Believe me, it is much better for him that he is inside and not outside right now." I was a bit relieved; sitting on the curb I tried to calm down. At times like this, one just looks around for an array of hope. Despite hesitating, I still asked him, whom I had now figured out that he was a police officer: "My brother and son are inside the police building to see my husband who is in custody. We brought a few things for my husband and I wrote a note. Do you think they will allow him to get them?" I don't know whether he really meant it, but he said, "Don't worry about it, he will get them."

My son and brother arrived half an hour later. Apparently, they had delivered the bag to someone at the entrance of the building, and they were told: "You can be 100% sure we're going to give it to him." They weren't allowed to see Gokhan, but were told that he was "fine." The feeling I remember from that day was that everyone was so upset and nobody felt like talking. Even when we arrived at my brother's home, we tried not to talk too much about it among us.

The next day I continued to search for criminal lawyers online. I even talked to the famous lawyer Celal Ulgen. But he politely refused, saying "There are other people who want me to take their cases. But my political situation is widely known, working with me can do you more harm than good." I thought that as a lawyer he knew that these cases were weak, they were a product of political hatred. So I didn't insist on my request. Apparently, he was very reluctant to take our case; perhaps out of fear, or maybe he couldn't reconcile these cases with his own political position or belief system. I don't know. To tell the truth, no lawyer was brave enough to take these cases during that time period. I think there was only one lawyer, Kemal Ucar, who didn't mind to take these cases. It was no surprise that he himself got imprisoned for some time, too. But I had not contacted him, actually I had not known him at that time anyhow.

My husband was a member of the union *Turk Egitim-Sen*[23]. I spoke to a close friend of Gokhan who was a member of the same union. I requested of him to contact the union on my behalf to allocate a lawyer to Gokhan. Normally, the union was supposed to allocate a lawyer to support its member, but they didn't accept my request, either.

I was afraid that they would torture Gokhan, but there was nothing I could do to stop it. I can't explain to you the desperation that I was going through, and I don't think you can truly understand it, either. I asked my father-in-law, "Please go to Caglayan Courthouse and give a petition to the prosecutor's office saying that we are worried that Gokhan is being tortured. That might frighten them and they might stop or at least lessen their torture". But my father-in-law pretty much ignored me, saying, "That won't help, not even a bit!" When I insisted on my request, he said "Okay" and after a few days he told me, "Well, I went to the courthouse, but the prosecutor was not in his office."

---

23 Abbreviation of *Turk Egitim Sendikasi* in Turkish, Union of Education Workers.

Country roads, take me home...to the place I belong!

It was such a difficult situation that I would have easily lost my mind if I didn't have my children. I was trying to stay strong for them. My son was aware of everything because he was old enough, but my daughter was very young. I was trying not to reflect any of this on her. When she was asking questions about what was going on, I was not necessarily telling her everything.

I couldn't help but read about the daily news on the internet every now and then. They were talking about tortures using bottles, Palestinian hanging, beating, and many other things. I was trying to push negative thoughts away but I just couldn't help it. I was going crazy with fear and anxiety. I've prayed and prayed and then prayed some more. My dear daughter was drawing pictures and writing notes on them: "Daddy, when are you coming back? I miss you so much! Please come quickly so we can go to our home together!"

In the midst of all these, I was also scared for myself, startled by every door and elevator sound. It was not uncommon for the police to arrest the wives of the men whom they had arrested earlier. What would my children do if that were to happen?

The next few days passed by looking for a lawyer and calling the Bar Association. I talked to a lot of lawyers who were experts in their fields. But no one agreed to take our case. It was either a direct "no" or just stalling.

I NEVER THOUGHT HE WOULD DIE...

When I called the Bar Association on Friday afternoon, I was told to call back at 8:00 pm. A week after Gokhan's arrest, the prosecutor finally requested a lawyer, and the lawyer's name would be revealed in the evening. I have to admit, I was a little hopeful. They had not let us see Gokhan so far, nor would they give us any information. But it would be easier to have some information about him through the lawyer. At least we would know what he was accused of.

I immediately called the lawyer whose name and phone number I got from the Bar that evening. But he didn't answer. Instead he texted, "I can't talk on the phone, text me using WhatsApp." Well, he was scared, too. I started writing one message after another. "Did you see my husband? If not, when will you see him? I'm very worried, please let me know." He first told me that he would go to the police station soon. Later, around midnight, he texted: "I couldn't see him today, I hope tomorrow morning."

The next day, in the afternoon, he wrote that he had

met with Gokhan. I read his message over and over again, and I felt like my heart was going to jump out of my chest. To make sure that I didn't misread it, I read it one more time. Yes, that was what he had said. He said he had seen Gokhan. I called him right away, but he didn't pick it up. I got the same text again: "Use WhatsApp." "No!" I wrote back. "I have too many questions in my mind, and I want to talk on the phone." He then accepted a call on WhatsApp. I called right away and asked: "Is my husband all right?"

"He is fine," he said. "He was a little depressed, but it felt good for him to talk to someone from outside."

"Please... can we meet face-to-face?"

"I can't do that. I'm not available."

"OK," I said, and I started asking my questions one after the other: "I suspect my husband was tortured. We had brought a bag for him with his medication and some clothes inside. Did he receive them?"

"They gave him his medication, but nothing else."

"What do you mean? Should I bring clothes again?"

"Yes, that would be good."

"OK, well... how about torture? Was there any sign of torture on his hands, face, or anywhere on his body?"

The lawyer was silent. After a few seconds, which seemed like a year to me, he said softly, "No."

"I want to file a complaint with the prosecutor's office," I said in a firm voice.

"Your husband's official statement is not taken yet. Things are still kind of chaotic, you better be patient and write the petition after some time."

The lawyer didn't intend to talk too long. In a hurry to hang up the phone, he then just said something, as if it was something unimportant: "By the way... your husband's eyeglasses were broken. If you have spare eyeglasses, can you bring them? He's having trouble seeing around. But don't forget to get permission from the prosecutor's office first."

That's when it felt like boiling water poured down on my head! My ears were ringing! I didn't even fully hear what he said after "broken glasses."

"How can they be broken?!" I said nervously. "His glasses were unbreakable with progressive transition lenses. Impossible to break, unless stamped on them!"

Another silence...

I could only say, "You said there was no torture."

He ended the conversation by saying, "You get

permission from the prosecutor's office and bring the glasses."

He was so young, inexperienced, and afraid. Or maybe it was just that he, too, believed Gokhan was guilty. I don't know; I couldn't get anything else from him.

Situations like this are very difficult. One part of you screams, "How could those glasses break if there was no torture?" And the other part tries to be optimistic, saying, "Maybe someone stepped on them by mistake while pushing him around." But no matter which way I looked at it, it didn't matter because there was nothing I could do about it! Yes, something was going on, but I couldn't do anything to prevent it. They would not allow me to see him, nor would they accept a petition that I wanted to submit to the prosecutor's office. All the reasons had ceased to exist. There was only one thing that I could do and I was doing that: Praying to God!

I had wounds in my mouth and on my face due to the severe stress at that time. It was as if I was in the middle of a quicksand, trying to survive. I was trying to reach for something, for someone to pull me out. All the doors were getting slammed in my face, but I was still knocking on them. I've never given up hope, prayers, and perseverance.

The Life and Legacy of Gokhan Acikkollu

I didn't know that day how Gokhan's glasses were broken. But later, after Gokhan died, I was going to learn from an interview given by the forensic expert Gurol Berber to journalist Ece Sevim Ozturk. One of those days when they took Gokhan to another room to question and torture him, one of the policemen swooped down on him as soon as he walked in and shouted, "Why are you looking at me!" When Gokhan turned his eyes away, the same policeman started to beat him, again shouting "Why don't you look at my eyes?" Then, many accusatory questions followed: "Did you give the coup order?! How many people were under your command?! What are their names?!" Another policeman in the room hit my husband on the back with his knee and when Gokhan fell to the ground they all began to kick and beat him. Gokhan tried to protect himself from the blows he was getting, it was then that his glasses fell on the floor and crushed. Gokhan told all of this to his cellmates when he was brought back to his cell afterward, battered.

After talking with the lawyer, I immediately called the Vatan Police Department and said that we were going to bring spare glasses for my husband. On the evening of that day, my brother went and delivered the glasses. The officer said to my brother, "Wait a minute, so I'll call and confirm that he is here." Apparently, at that time, Gokhan had been taken to a medical checkup. My brother asked, "Can I wait here and give the glasses to him myself?" But his request was not accepted. So my brother waited in the front yard of the building. After a while, when a police van approached the building, my brother walked in that direction. It was then that he saw my husband getting out of the vehicle in handcuffs, together with some other detainees. Since the police wouldn't let my brother to come any closer, my brother could see Gokhan only from afar, but Gokhan was able to see him, too, and tried to wave his hand as much as he can. That was the last time anyone in our family saw my husband, even though for a few seconds.

I was very afraid and worried for Gokhan, but the possibility of his death did not even cross my mind. I knew that he had a very sensitive soul and a fragile body. I was afraid that if he were to stay in prison for a long time, that would cause a serious damage to his health and he couldn't possibly get over the trauma. But I never thought he would die.

Even though we had a lawyer now, nothing had changed. We still could not get any information related to Gokhan, his official statement was still not taken, and the uncertainty still continued.

The Life and Legacy of Gokhan Acikkollu

On Wednesday, August 3rd, exactly four days after our first meeting, I received a new text message from the Bar Association's lawyer which read as "I talked to your husband in person!" I called him right away. He didn't pick up. After a while, I called again. He didn't answer again. I texted him: "Please, let's meet face-to-face just this once. Give me an address and I'll come to your office." In response, he wrote, "I am not using the office." I insisted, "Then tell me when you're going to the police building. I can meet with you in front of the building. We can talk a little bit, please?" Even though I insisted, he just didn't accept it. He then answered my phone, again using WhatsApp. I was very curious about my husband's condition. When the lawyer told me that Gokhan's statement had not been taken yet, I just couldn't take it anymore and asked in anger: "But why?! It has been 10 days! Why are they still not taking his statement?" Instead of saying something clearly, the lawyer asked me: "Did your husband have any other duties other than being a teacher?! They're looking into that."

The only thing that warmed my heart about that meeting was the note that Gokhan sent with the lawyer: "Tell my wife I love her very much!". This would be the last message I got from him. And it was so precious to me. I told the lawyer in excitement: "Please tell Gokhan that I love him very much, too! We love him very much and no matter what happens, we will stand by him until the end!"

My message probably never got to him. In normal life, like most Turkish families, we were not people who expressed their love to each other every day. Precisely because of that, and in the middle of everything that he was going through, that he sent me that note was very precious.

As I told you, I had been frantically looking for a lawyer since my husband was taken into custody. I had reached out to most of them, and talked to them in this way or that way. One of the lawyers was an expert in his field with an agile mind. The day after I met with the Bar's lawyer, on the afternoon of Thursday, August 4th, I met with that other lawyer at a café. He listened to me patiently and said, "I will meet with your husband tomorrow afternoon. Then I will decide whether I will take the case or not."

But unfortunately, that meeting on the next day would not happen!

The Life and Legacy of Gokhan Acikkollu

"MOM, WHAT IS FORENSICS?"

Yes, my biggest concern was that Gokhan had been in custody for so many days. But that wasn't all I was concerned about. Without him, even though my family was supportive, all the other burden was on my shoulders. My daily responsibilities were still there. I was knocking on the doors of lawyers every day, meanwhile I was also looking for a new school for my children whose schools were shut down by the government.

My son was going to begin his senior year in high school and prepare for the coming college entrance exams. It was a critical year, and I was looking for a school that would not only be within our budget but would also provide a good education. I told you earlier, Fatih was very good with electronics and computers just like his father, and naturally he had a dream of becoming a computer engineer. But all those things that have happened recently had changed him as well as all of us, and he decided to study law. He wasn't a very social kid, but he had a friend he'd been close with since middle school, and we talked to his parents and decided to enroll them in the same high school because it would be easier for them to get used to it. There was a new high school in Umraniye which was giving regular high school education and also preparing

Country roads, take me home...to the place I belong!

students for the college entrance exam. And my daughter would go to the elementary school in our neighborhood.

August 5th, 2016...It was Friday...We were still staying with my brothers on the European side of Istanbul. That day we got up early in the morning and hit the road to enroll Fatih in the new school. On Fridays, traffic in Istanbul is such a mess. We had left early so we wouldn't be late for the school, but the traffic was jammed up already until we arrived from Beylikduzu to the Bosphorus Bridge. Right when we had entered the bridge, my phone rang. Someone calling from an unknown number said, "Ma'am, you need to come to Haseki hospital immediately!" I got scared and panicked. "What's the matter? Is my husband in a coma or something?" The answer was ice-cold: "I can't give any other information, come urgently!" I got so scared that my heart missed a beat. I begged: "Please tell me what happened? I'll die of anxiety until I get there!" It felt like I was talking to a robot and not a human being. "I don't know," said the voice on the other hand of the line and hung up the phone on my face.

We had just entered the bridge; it was going to take us hours to get back. I immediately called my other brother: "Please go to Haseki Hospital now! Call me from there, I want to hear that Gokhan is fine."

Meanwhile, we crossed the Bosphorus Bridge only to turn back, but there was such a traffic! You feel so helpless in these situations! I wish we had wings and could fly to Haseki. Inside the car, we were as silent as the graveyard. The cars were moving so slowly, bumper to bumper. I wanted to open the car window and shout, "For the love of God, give way!" It was an hour later when I was called again: "Have you arrived?" the voice across the line asked. "No," I said helplessly. "There's traffic, we're on our way!" I hung up and hastily called my brother again and said, "Where are you?" They were about to enter through the door of the hospital, and I told them to find out what was going on.

I was praying constantly. If only the traffic jam were to break up! If only I could get to Haseki Hospital as soon as possible! Probably Gokhan had a blood sugar spike, if only it had returned to normal levels! If only he was safe and healthy, and I could say "Thank God!" Please, My Lord, please! For the sake of the holiness of the day of Friday, for the sake of your loved ones! Please!

Half an hour later, my phone rang again. I answered it right away. This time they said: "Come to the Forensics Medicine Office immediately!" That moment!!! As if hundreds of tiny needles were poked into every inch of my body! The August heat turned into ice-cold. The last piece of hope I had inside me was crushed! "Why?" I asked with fear. "You had said to come to the Haseki Hospital!" The voice on the line said, "No, not the hospital, Forensic Medicine! Hurry up!" The phone went dead again. I was left aghast! My hands were trembling as I called my brother again. I only said, "Go to the Forensic Medicine!" and hung up before he could even ask a question.

As someone who worked in the healthcare industry for many years, I knew the Forensic Medicine Office very well and what it meant. But it wasn't easy to accept the underlying message when it involved your loved ones. I tried to calm down. "Maybe," I thought, "Maybe they are using that place to run some tests during the state of emergency." When the possibility of his death came to my mind and when I caught myself thinking along "Could he really be dead?", I was trying to throw that thought away: "I hope I'm wrong. Please Lord, let me be wrong! Please!"

My brother and I made eye contact for a moment. Both of us were probably thinking about the same things, we were pretty much speechless. My son was pressing me from the back seat: "Mom, mom, what's the forensic office? What are they doing there?" One of the most difficult questions for a mother to answer. I gave him explanations, hoping to be right about them: "They are running blood tests over there sometimes. Also if one gets food poisoning or something like that, they might take him there." I pretty much told him whatever came to my mind, meanwhile biting my lips not to start crying all of a sudden. I don't know how convinced my son was, but he didn't ask any more questions and a deep silence fell in the car again.

I was secretly wiping away my tears and constantly praying. I just couldn't wait, but the traffic was moving so slowly. I was about to go crazy!

"YOU KILLED HIM!"

The road was never ending. Finally, exactly three hours after we received the first call in the morning, we reached the Forensic Medicine Office in Yenibosna, around 12:30 pm. On the way, I had called Gokhan's parents and informed them of the situation and told them to come to that office. Their house was nearby, so they arrived right after us.

When I got out of the car, I stopped and looked at the building for a moment. I was still trying to fool myself and thinking, "They are just running some tests here during the state of emergency. Probably Gokhan got a diabetic coma and they brought him here." Could this cold building be hiding the lifeless body of the man I love? Even though that feeling had been probing me over and over again and up to my marrow, I had never dwelt on it. He just couldn't be dead!

They had told us to come urgently, but they kept us waiting outside for one and a half hours. I dialed the number that had called me earlier in the morning and said that we arrived. They said, "We will let you know." But it was as if the time had stopped and the entire world had collapsed on me. People around were talking, saying things, but I could not even detect the sounds. I sat down on the pavement, my body couldn't take the stress of waiting any longer. Then someone came out of the building and shouted, "Gokhan Acikkollu's relatives should come in!" I jumped forward in excitement, but my brothers stopped me, saying "We don't know what we will face, it is better if we go in first."

As my brothers entered, I turned around and looked at Gokhan's family, who were waiting behind. I think I resented when I noticed that his brother, who was a police officer, didn't make any attempt to get in, but I didn't dwell on it. As long as my Gokhan was safe and sound, nothing else mattered. My son and I were left behind, waiting like sheep to be slaughtered. Oh, my dear son...all his life, he has lived his feelings inside. And there, he didn't say a word; he just remained silent and waited together with me.

It had been fourteen days. Fourteen days and nights when we couldn't see Gokhan or hear his voice! Two weeks on edge, and like a deep void, without knowing what was going to happen. Neither could Gokhan tell us about his situation during this time, nor could we comfort him. He lived everything alone in his cell, and we were all alone outside.

While I was thinking about all this, I was constantly looking at the clock and getting more and more impatient. If only my brothers came out and said, "He was in a diabetic coma, but he's fine now!" Or if only he were here for some medical tests. I wanted to hear things like that! God, please! Death wouldn't befit him, my beloved husband!

It must be about 30-45 minutes later, my brothers came out and we rushed to them, asking "What is it?" I was looking for some good news, a smile on their faces. But neither of them was smiling. They even averted their eyes from us. Only one sentence came out of my brother's mouth that I wish I had never heard: "I am very sorry, we've lost Gokhan!"

…

Country roads, take me home...to the place I belong!

I had never experienced anything like this in my life. I was literally dumbstruck. I couldn't stand on my feet and held on to my brother so I wouldn't fall. Then I began yelling and screaming, "They killed him! They killed Gokhan! He was fine 2 weeks ago, they killed him!" My son was like frozen, he couldn't even cry, my poor child. My brothers were trying to silence me but I was not going to be silent! I had just lost my husband, the pillar of my home, the father of my children; what else was there left to lose? There was a sliding door in front of the building, and I held on to its bars and yelled, "He was just a teacher! My husband wasn't a terrorist! You killed him! You are the real terrorists!" I just couldn't calm down! I couldn't accept it! My brother got scared and said "For God's sake, stop it! Police is everywhere, they will take you in, too!"

It was not only the police who was around, there were also journalists, but none of them was interested in reporting on our or anyone else's grievance. Although my brother told me to be quiet, he couldn't stand it himself and told them: "If you're looking for a news, here's the real news! I dare you to write our story! The government killed its own citizen while he was in custody!" Nobody made a single sound. One or two of them came nearby and got a phone number, that's it!

Apparently, after a long time, they found and talked

to my parents-in-law. Did they report Gokhan's death as news afterward? Of course, they did. For example, the rag called *Yeni Safak* newspaper made a headline that was far from reality, compassion, and conscience: "One of the leaders of the coup died of diabetic coma." Another one reported Gokhan as "The coup plotter is buried without a ceremony."

Yeni Akit Daily Newspaper August 8, 2016

Darbeci 'öğretmen' imamsız gömüldü

The putschist teacher buried without [a prayer led by] an imam.

While I was crying there desperately, an old man walked up towards me. Apparently, he was the father of a captain who was killed on the night of July 15th. He said sadly, "I am sorry for your loss." He said that he was waiting in front of this building for the last 20 days to get his son's dead body. His son was declared a traitor without any trial, and they wouldn't even give his dead body to his father. The captain had two little children. The old man said, "The city authorities want to bury my son in the *Cemetery of Traitors*. And they sent word from my hometown in order not to bring my son there, either. I don't know what to do, so if I can get his body, I'm going to bury my son in the backyard of my house." I felt very sorry for him, too.

The burial plot with a sign reading "Cemetery of Traitors" in Turkish at its entrance.

We were sitting around a table in a cafeteria-like place, waiting helplessly. My brothers had gone to get the corpse (how strange it was to talk about the man you love as "corpse" all of a sudden). After a while they came back, saying that they are not giving Gokhan's dead body! It was a second shock for me! "But why?" I asked. As if murdering Gokhan wasn't enough, they had told my brothers that they were going to bury him in the so-called traitors' cemetery. To elaborate, they would take my Gokhan in a body bag and throw it into a hole and cover it up with dirt without washing, shrouding, and without the funeral prayer! Without even allowing us to attend! It turns out that it was a luxury to be able to grieve after your loved one's death. Fear was added now to the deep pain we had been through. As if murdering my husband wasn't enough, they would not even let us take his body, and they would bury him as a traitor!

My brothers' courage was truly admirable. In a time period when even those who said "Hi" to Hizmet members were labeled as "terrorist", when Gokhan's own parents and brother were afraid and stood back, my brothers talked to police and insisted to get Gokhan's body. At one point, my brothers told the police officers, "Look, Gokhan's brother is a police officer too, he's serving our country. Why are you giving us such a hard time? He has already passed away!" My brother-in-law somehow heard this and after a few minutes he came next to my brothers, criticizing "Why did you tell them that I am a police officer?" Upon hearing that, I got disappointed and hurt, one more time. After all, my brothers could have been arrested that day, but they rushed in to get Gokhan's body, taking all the risks.

Unfortunately, we didn't even have the luxury of

grieving properly for Gokhan. We couldn't save his life and now we were concerned about getting his dead body. The people that we were dealing with had no conscience whatsoever. When I yelled at them, "How can you declare someone a terrorist when his statement is not even taken, let alone appearing in the court and being sentenced?!" I think that made some kind of sense for them because this time instead of simply saying "No", they told us: "Then go and get proper documents from the prosecutor's office!"

My brothers rushed to the office of the prosecutor-in-charge and they didn't come back for a long time. Apparently, the prosecutor said "What nonsense is that? There's no need for any extra paperwork, there is a standard procedure to follow. Tell them to give you the corpse!" But when those officials in the Forensic Medicine insisted not to give Gokhan's body to us, my brothers went back to the prosecutor who then said: "OK then, go to the Counter-Terrorism Police Directorate and get a signed document indicating that his statement has not been taken yet."

The authorities, who were competing with each other to arrest a teacher who had not committed any crime whatsoever, were now walking away from their responsibilities when it involved to hand over Gokhan's body. Instead of preparing a document, the Counter-Terrorism Directorate passed the buck to the Directorate of Cemeteries and said, "Let them send us an official document indicating that they are willing to bury this body, and we will respond to them." But it was also impossible to reach an official from the Directorate of Cemeteries. The assistant director, whom we finally managed to talk to, told us that the director is on annual leave and he'll be back on Monday.

We understood that this nonsense would go on, and the bureaucracy would keep us busy for days. They were going to keep my Gokhan waiting in that cold morgue. It was then that my brother offered me either of two things to do. "Either Gokhan's own family can take their son to Kars, or we will take him to our village in Konya and have a funeral there." I couldn't let them take Gokhan to Kars and bury him there! Even his parents hadn't been to Kars for decades. I said, "Let's bring him to Konya!" And when I asked Gokhan's parents for their consent, they said, "Yes, that would be more appropriate." But right then, one of Gokhan's relatives intervened, "I have a friend who is a prosecutor. Let me ask him, maybe he can help." I didn't have much hope, but we decided to wait for him to contact his friend, as Gokhan's parents were not truly pleased with the idea of their son to be buried in Konya, so far from Istanbul. So, Gokhan's body had to wait one more day at the cold morgue.

Sometimes I would think, "On horrible days like this, would people who get the very sad news lose their minds? Would they still be able to continue with their consciousness of the Lord? Would they continue with their regular daily prayers? Or would this pain make them forget their prayers? Would the pain take away the consciousness?" My Lord had allowed me to go through this test on that day. When I was in front of the Forensic Medicine building, constantly crying and dealing with these problems, I somehow turned to my sister and said, "What time is it? Is prayer time passing?" There was a parking lot behind the building, and I remember laying down the prayer rug that I always keep in the car and offering my afternoon prayer.

TO THIS DAY, I STILL CAN'T ACCEPT THE WAY HE DIED

It was our first evening at home without Gokhan. The house was packed with relatives, some of them crying, others reciting Qur'an and praying. I was exhausted, crying, writhing in pain, couldn't eat or drink anything. When I couldn't cry anymore, I was resting a bit and then crying more. At some point, I couldn't take it anymore and had lain on the couch. But the moment I was closing my eyes, I was seeing Gokhan in front of me. One of the close relatives had taken my daughter out of the house to keep her away from that mournful atmosphere and I had not even noticed where my son was that evening. When I look back, it's been six years now. Death is God's will and command, of course I accept it. But to this day I still cannot accept the way Gokhan died.

I didn't sleep that night at all. The next day, all day long, we waited for a news from my father-in-law. They were grieving in their home; we were in ours. For eighteen years, there was not even a slightest disagreement between us. But now, I was very upset and angry. Maybe they were right from their point of view, but I expected them to do more than just shed tears. If they had tried to do their best, if they had supported me while I was trying to find a lawyer, if they had at least accepted to file a petition with the prosecutor upon my insistence…if they hadn't said, "There wouldn't be torture in this day and age"…if my brother-in-law had not stepped back and said, "Keep me out of this!" Well, if all these had not happened, would Gokhan be alive today? Probably not! According to our faith, we believe that God's decree regarding the time of one's death cannot be deferred. I just wish that Gokhan's

Country roads, take me home...to the place I belong!

family members would have done everything they could. They neither rushed around to find a lawyer for their son, nor did they go to the prosecutor's office to file a petition in order to protect him... And now, it was too late for all of this.

That day, late in the afternoon, we got the news that the other prosecutor couldn't help the situation, either. So, early Sunday morning, my brothers went and took Gokhan's body. Meanwhile, the officials caused even more trouble. The body needed to be prepared with some chemicals to preserve it, because we had to take him in the summer heat to Konya, which was 700 kilometers away from Istanbul. It was a standard procedure, but the officials refused to do it for him. Why? You know why! My brother insisted, "At least give us the name of the chemical, show us how to do it, and we'll take care of it." At last, someone with some kind of conscience gave him the chemicals and showed him how to do it. My brother prepared the body with his own hands. But then they kept us waiting a long time, again. Then, they put his body inside a nonstandard coffin. And why was that? "Because the Istanbul Metropolitan Municipality decided not to allocate a coffin with its logo on it!" Gokhan had served his country for so many years and paid his taxes regularly. In return, not only he was murdered by his government, but that same government did not even allocate a coffin for his corpse.

Photo showing the coffin of Acikkollu in the car of a family member, because the local government did not allocate a hearse for the trip from Istanbul to Konya (700 km).

By noon, they brought Gokhan to my brother's house that we were staying. There was a green piece of cloth over the coffin. They had reclined the seats of my brother's Citroen car in order to fit the coffin inside it. My brothers' apartment was on the first floor of the building. I looked out of the window. It was only two weeks ago when I had seen Gokhan at the train station, strong and healthy. He was now lying lifeless inside a coffin covered

Country roads, take me home...to the place I belong!

with a piece of green cloth. It was a Friday when we had seen each other last time. And two weeks later, on another Friday, I had learned that he died.

My son seemed to have had his feelings removed. I looked at him every now and then; he wasn't crying at all. I was worried, so I asked my nephew, "Why doesn't he even cry?" "No, auntie, he cries." he said, "he just doesn't cry in front of you." There is a saying that no matter how old a person is, he grows up when his father dies. And I was going to perceive this bitter truth when my father passed away two and a half years after Gokhan's death. My dear son Fatih apparently had hugged his cousin and cried for half an hour when he saw his father's coffin, But he was acting calm around me in order not to upset me.

There is one more thing I remember about that day which still hurts me to this day. We had a WhatsApp group with friends we had been in touch since high school. One of them called me, someone I thought was "one of my best friends." We had shared a bunk bed in high school for four years, went to college in the same city, and worked at the same hospital for five years. We were like sisters. She asked: "Tulay, I've heard that Gokhan is dead, is that correct?" Oh, how much I would have wanted to be able to say that it was not correct! But unfortunately it was. She just said, "My condolences," and immediately hung up the phone! Just like that! Soon after, I started getting notifications on my phone. One by one, people in that WhatsApp group left the group, as if they were running from plague. And that friend of mine, whom I had considered like a sister to me…well, we have never talked to each other again, since that day.

Gokhan's parents soon arrived, we were about to set off for Konya. Gokhan's brother did not show up. His parents said, "He couldn't make it." It was my brothers who had dealt with everything related to the funeral.

My brother, alone in the car with the coffin, left at once. He was afraid that the police could cause even more trouble. During those days, we were afraid of everything. Those evil people could do every evil act during those days! We were worried that they wouldn't allow us to bury Gokhan in the cemetery in Konya, either. After what we had been through, we did not know what was going to happen in Konya. Soon, my children and I took the road, in my sister's car.

FAREWELLS ARE DIFFICULT

While we were on our way to Konya, my parents searched for a burial site. They talked to the mayor of our small town and arranged a burial site, but when they went to

Country roads, take me home...to the place I belong!

the county hall to get help digging the grave, they were told that heir excavator was broken. They went to another county near us hoping they can get help from them, but it turned out their excavator was broken, too! Well, it didn't need to be a genius to figure out that the county administrations would not help us!

We had a relative living around. Once, he had stayed in our house in Istanbul for two weeks when his father was in a hospital's intensive care unit. He helped out to find an excavator to dig the grave. We paid for the cost of the equipment and labor.

My dear Gokhan was kept in a morgue near my father's house. It was only a few weeks ago that all of us were in this house, happily. Hard to accept it, but it was time to say goodbye. His parents didn't want to come to the morgue because they didn't want to see their son like that. We went as a family. We took turns to enter into the room and said goodbye to our dear Gokhan.

I looked at his face with love; it was still bright and smiling. Oh, how hard it was to see my loved one for that last time! There seemed to be a calmness on his face, as if to say, "I'm free of the troubles of this world now! Good luck to you!" I was burning inside. I touched his face with my hand, caressed. I said *"Hakkini helal et"*[24] three times. My Lord be my witness, I was pleased with his companionship. I guess I stayed in the room a bit long, so my sister came inside, worried. As I was leaving, I turned around and looked at his innocent face again and again. I don't know if it was only me who thought that his face looked extraordinarily bright, but our relative who washed the body to prepare for the funeral later said "I'm sure he died a martyr, his body was almost weightless".

After me, my son said his goodbyes to his father. But he never told me how he did that. Afterwards, I asked him a few times about the details, but he wouldn't say a thing.

My aunt and father had been cross with each other for the last 40 years. They had not seen or talked to each other for that very long time. I don't exactly know why, even they probably had forgotten the reason. Some years ago, even when my father went to her home to make peace right before his pilgrimage journey to Mecca, my aunt had not accepted that peace offer. But now, before leaving this world, my Gokhan accomplished what seemed to be impossible to do: He reunited my father and aunt, because my aunt came to our house after decades!

---

24 Phrase in Turkish, meaning, "Please forgive me for all my faults towards you with or without knowing. Let's please make a peace between our hearts forever."

Country roads, take me home...to the place I belong!

The funeral prayer was held, and we all sincerely said our goodbyes to Gokhan one last time. After the prayer, when we were asked what we have thought of him, we all said together: "May our Lord bear witness that we testify that he was a good person!"

A reporter from pro-government media, Dogan News Agency, came to the funeral with his camera. We didn't notice him around but when one of our relatives saw him, he told the reporter not to take any pictures and asked him to leave. So far, they had only written lies and slanders about us. The next day, they published another news on their media channel, again full of lies.

Milliyet Daily Newspaper August 8, 2016
Eşinin memleketinde imamsız gömüldü

Buried in his wife's hometown without [a prayer led by] an imam.

Women were waiting on the sidelines while the men shoveled dirt into the grave. At one point, I collapsed to the ground because my legs could no longer carry me. After the burial was over and passages from Quran were recited, I walked and crouched down next to the head of the grave. I caressed his grave in tears and prayed. At 41 years of age, I cried that day more than I had ever cried in my life.

There were about forty people at the funeral. Later, Ismet Macit, a scholar and author, published a post on his social media account comparing Gokhan's situation to that of Osman bin Affan[25]. I would like to share with you that article upon reading which I've found some consolation.

Osman bin Affan and Teacher Gokhan

Gokhan was a teacher who had devoted his life to spread knowledge and wisdom to his students.

After the damned coup attempt, to this day the perpetrators of which are unknown, the Hizmet movement has been used as

---

25 Osman bin Affan (579 – 656) was one of the companions of Prophet Muhammad (Peace be upon Him). He was the fourth person to embrace Islam. He played a major role in early Islamic history as he ruled as the third Caliph for 12 years between 644-656. He is known for having ordered the compilation of the first standard version of the Quran.

Country roads, take me home…to the place I belong!

a scapegoat and Gokhan had been detained, totally unaware of anything related to the coup. He was diabetic. He was able to survive the inhumane practices in the prison cell only for 13 days. His body was not warm anymore when he had come out of the prison…it was ice cold, with marks of beatings.

He was declared a coup plotter. But he was only in custody. He was not officially questioned, his statement was not taken, he was not officially charged with anything, he was not put on trial yet, and definitely he was not found guilty of any crime by the court. He was just one of the hundreds of thousands of well-educated young people who was declared a "coup plotter" by the society into which systematic anger and hatred has been pumped for a long time.

Gokhan died in prison…his religious funeral ceremony was not led by a mosque official on government payroll. He was not allowed to be buried in Istanbul, where he was living with his family, but instead in his wife's hometown of Konya. One of his relatives led his funeral ceremony.

I remembered the funeral of Osman bin Affan. A mob that was deceived by Ibn-i Sebe, had martyred our beloved Osman. The mob had not allowed his body to be buried for two days.

Some mob members had attacked his funeral, tried to stone his body and throw him out of his coffin. According to Vakidi's narration, when Osman's body was placed on the altar for prayer, a vile man called Umeyr ibn-i Dabi jumped on him and broke one of his rib bones, saying "That is what you get for you had imprisoned a man from the Dabi tribe and kept him in prison until he died!" The mob rebels went even further and demanded that Osman be buried in the Jewish cemetery in Deyri Sin.

These bandits said that Osman should not be buried inside the Baqi[26] cemetery. So they buried him outside the walls of the Baqi cemetery, under a few palm trees in the neighborhood of Hashi Kev-Keb.

Around only 15 people attended his funeral in the evening darkness. He had served as the caliph for 12 years. He was one of the ten companions of the Prophet Muhammad (sallallahu aleyhi ve sellem) who were given the good news during their lifetime that they will be awarded Heaven. He had married Ruqayyah, and after her death, he had married her sister Umm Kulthum. Both of them were the daughters of Prophet Muhammad (sallallahu aleyhi ve sellem). This is why he was titled as Zinnurayn (the bearer of two blessed lights). Even the angels were shy in his presence.

Gokhan said goodbye to his short life in this world, sharing the same fate of Osman bin Affan. May Allah bring them together in the Hereafter. May our Lord give patience to Gokhan's grieving family. Please pray for Gokhan.

---

26 An Islamic cemetery in Medina, Saudi Arabia. It was the first Islamic cemetery, containing graves of many of the Prophet Muhammad's (Peace be upon Him) family and companions.

Country roads, take me home…to the place I belong!

As for the mindset that murdered Teacher Gokhan and as for those who have chosen to be silent in the face of this murder!

May the Lord overcome you all!

I wasn't a person who easily cried, nor was I someone who could express her feelings easily. About two and a half years after Gokhan's death, far away from homeland, I would be torn to pieces once again when I received the news of my father's death. When a friend of mine came to support me that day, she put a pillow in my hand and said, "Think of this pillow as your father and express your feelings to him," I hugged the pillow and cried my lungs out.

I could see now clearly what it meant to have such an intense grief that it resonated in every cell of my body. I couldn't even breathe. It had been two days since we hid Gokhan in his grave, but I was still feeling suffocated. I was overwhelmed, I was drowning! The mayor of our small town came to our home. Apparently, the district governor had scolded him for not informing him about the funeral. The mayor told him: "It is quite often that we have a funeral for someone who died in Istanbul and brought here. I just followed the standard procedure and let them bury him since they had the proper death certificate." The governor replied: "But this was different, wasn't it? You should have let me know!"

When I heard that, I couldn't breathe anymore. I was so scared. I said, "Oh, my God! They're going to dig up his body to bury him somewhere else! They will begrudge even a grave to us." I couldn't control shivering and nonstop crying. My parents got so worried that they took me to the emergency service of a hospital around. For a while, I dragged myself around like a living dead.

Chapter 5

Seeking justice,

by any means necessary...

The Life and Legacy of Gokhan Acikkollu

I'VE STARTED TO DIG A WELL WITH A NEEDLE!

A week after laying Gokhan to rest, we returned to Istanbul with my brothers and sisters. We did not go to our home immediately, we had decided to stay in my brother's house for a while. Meanwhile, I had already talked to the lawyer. I was going to open a murder case without wasting time, and would hold those who murdered my husband accountable before the law, if of course, the rule of law still existed.

We could not continue with the lawyer I had previously hired. He was working on the cases of other people who stayed in the same cell with Gokhan, and after Gokhan's death, several of them wrote petitions, stating that they wanted to testify that my husband was "severely tortured" while being detained. I didn't know about this until later when their petitions were added to our case file. Since the lawyer I had hired was also their lawyer, he thought that it would involve a concurrent conflict of interest and didn't want to take our case.

August 12, 2016… One day after I returned to Istanbul, I went to the Murder Bureau of the Gayrettepe Public Order Division and gave a statement as complainant and filed a formal complaint. The police would investigate the evidence, prepare a murder file and send it to the prosecutor's office.

This process took a long time. In the following days, I called them frequently, but every time I got the same answer: "We are still getting the statements of the corresponding people." According to what they said, they were taking statements from those who were in custody together with Gokhan that day, from the doctors (who themselves were also detained) who performed the first aid on my husband, from the police officers on duty that night, and from the members of the paramedic emergency team which later stepped in. They also told me that it would take a long time to download the video footage of the last 13 days from the server in the police station. Pretty much they were saying: "It will take a very long time to prepare the case file."

I called the police often and asked if the file had been sent to the prosecutor's office yet. Even though we did not know how accurate and satisfying the file would be, at least the first step would have been taken.

The Life and Legacy of Gokhan Acikkollu

Homicide Branch Office in Gayrettepe, Istanbul

Plaintiff Statement of Tulay Acikkollu

August 12, 2016

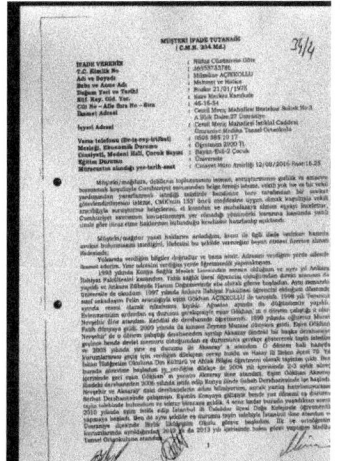
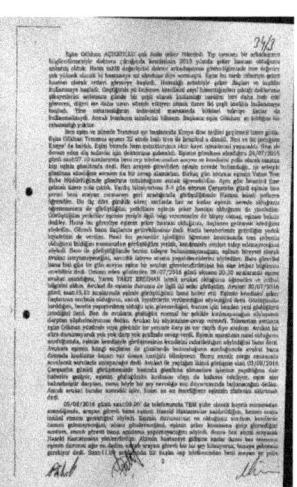
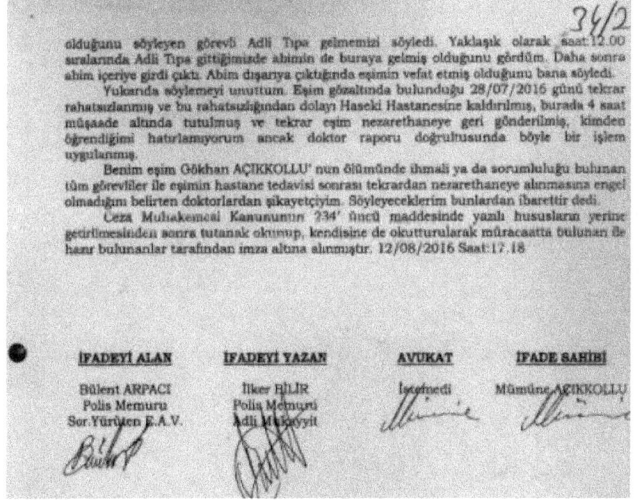

Seeking justice, by any means necessary…

"Hereby I lodge a complaint about all those who have neglected their duties and who are responsible for my husband Gokhan Acikkollu's death, including the doctors who have stated that there was no problem for the patient to continue to stay in detention after they had seen his condition during their medical checks."

It was written in the police records that Gokhan had died after being taken to the hospital by ambulance and after the emergency medical intervention performed there. But Forensic Medicine specialist Professor Dr. Haluk Ince, who was detained at that time and staying in the same ward together with Gokhan said in his statement: *"When I performed CPR on him, he was already dead."*

Counter-Terrorism Branch Office

Police Statement of Forensic Specialist, Professor Haluk İnce, MD

August 5, 2016

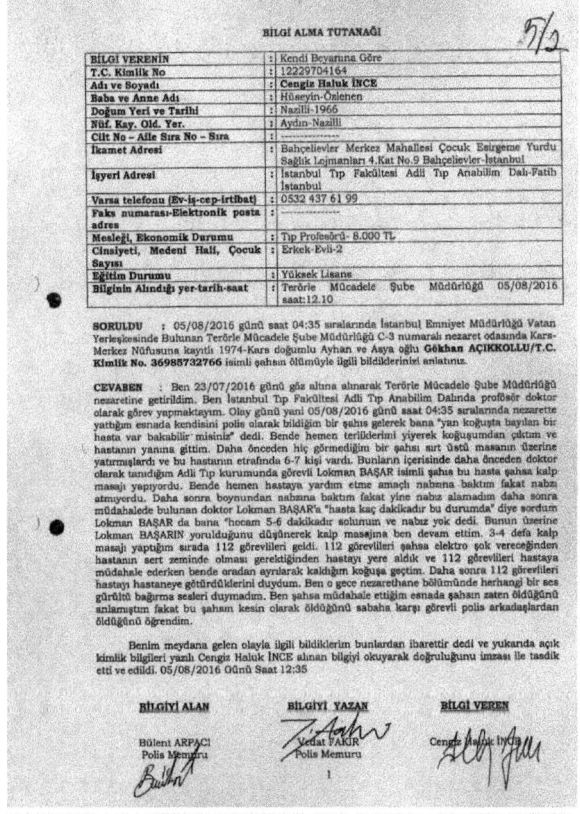

"I was taken in custody on July 23, 2016. On August 5, 2016 a police officer came to the cell where I was staying around 4:35

Seeking justice, by any means necessary...

a.m. in the morning and asked for my help for a medical emergency situation in the adjacent cell. When I went to the adjacent cell, I saw that Lokman Basar, MD [who was also detained at that time,] was performing CPR on someone. I checked the pulse on his wrist and neck. There was no pulse. Doctor Basar said that there is no pulse or breathing since 5-6 minutes. I continued with the CPR for some time...it was clear that the person had already died."

Also, the reports of the paramedic emergency team disprove the police reports and state that they came to the police station and continued with the CPR, but *"the person did not respond to the resuscitation efforts."* Of course, I didn't know any of this at the time.

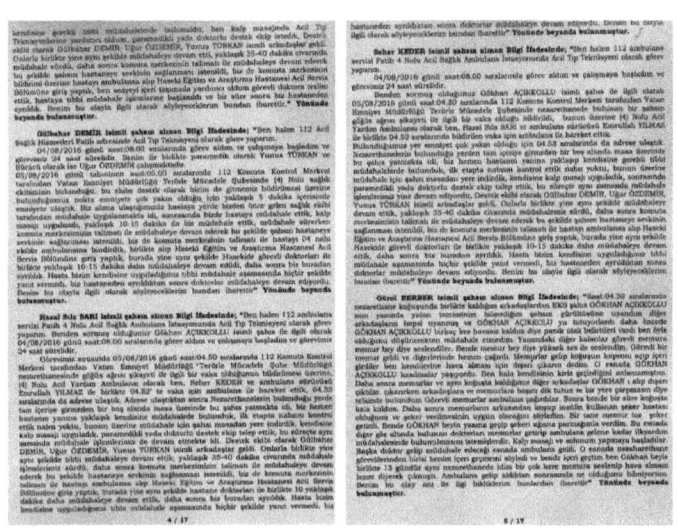

Police Statement of Gulbahar Demir, Emergency Medical Technician

"...during the CPR and the medical emergency process, we have noted that there was no response from the patient, whatsoever."

Police Statement of Hazal Sila Sari, Emergency Medical Technician

"After we arrived at the scene, we immediately checked for the pulse. He had no pulse. ...during the CPR and the medical emergency process, we have noted that there was no response from the patient, whatsoever."

Police Statement of Seher Keder, Emergency Medical Technician

"After we arrived at the scene, we immediately checked for the pulse. He had no pulse. ...during the CPR and the medical emergency process, we have noted that there was no response from the patient, whatsoever."

One week had passed after my last telephone call when I learned that the case was finally given to a prosecutor named Burhan Görgülü. Meanwhile, it took about one month to get the autopsy results. But interestingly, instead of sending the results to the prosecutor's office, they sent them to the Forensic Medicine Institute's Board of Experts. Why, you may ask? Because they could not state

Seeking justice, by any means necessary...

in their reports that "*Gokhan Acikkollu died of torture,*" so instead they referred the results to the superior board on the ground that they "*couldn't detect it.*" Well, they were uncertain about it, but for some unknown reason, the Board of Experts hastily prepared a document indicating that "*he died of a heart attack,*" and sent it to the prosecutor's office.

The Life and Legacy of Gokhan Acikkollu

Report of the Forensic Medicine Institute's Board of Experts

November 23, 2016

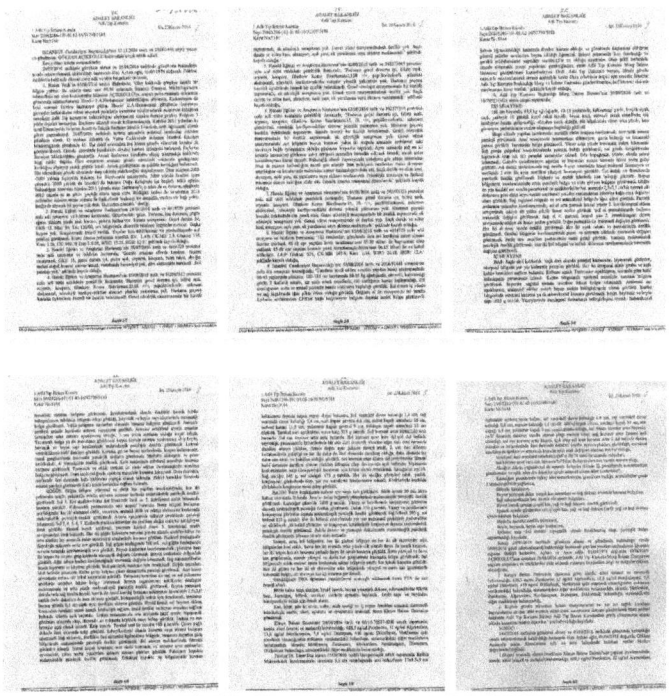

Seeking justice, by any means necessary...

The page of the report of the Forensic Medicine Institute's Board of Experts with the names of the doctors who prepared the report, concluding that Acikkollu died of a heart attack.

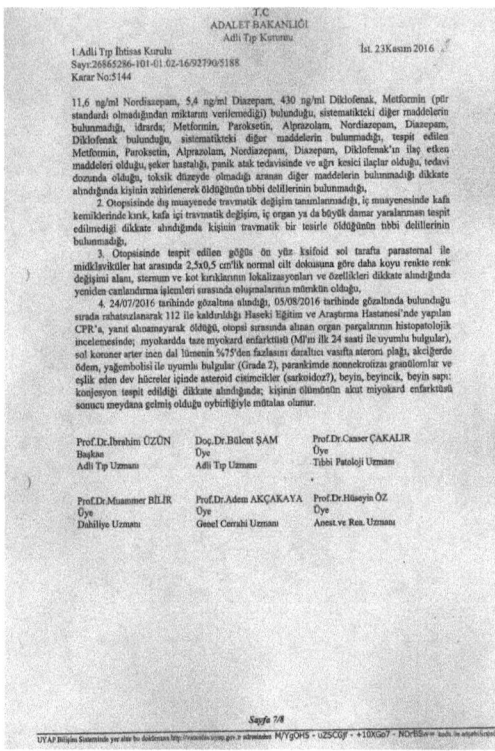

Even though I requested a copy of my husband's autopsy report from the Forensic Medicine Institute many times, they would not give it to me, saying "We will send it to the prosecutor's office." However, by law, the report should have been given to the next of kin upon request along with the photos taken during the autopsy. Even though we could get the report from the prosecutor's file afterward, we have never seen the autopsy photos. Either they were never given to the prosecutor's office by the Forensic Medicine Institute or the prosecutor hid them from us.

I had hired a lawyer, but I was personally following every step. I was even one step ahead of the lawyer. I was taking notes regularly: "Let's ask from the prosecutor's office for the video footage records in the police station. How was the general setting in the cell? How was it in the interrogation room? Did my husband have access to the diabetes medication when he needed it? If yes, at what time of the day did they give it to him? In what doses? Since food is very important in diabetic patients, was he given his daily meals on time? What kind of meals?" We had requested the information related to all these questions and many more, but have not been given an answer for any of them. We would learn much later, and only from his cellmates, that the detainees were not even given enough water to drink so that they would not use the toilet too much.

Seeking justice, by any means necessary…

FLOOR 4: THE TORTURE ROOM!

Since the morning of July 24, when I received that phone call and learned that Gokhan had been taken into custody, I have done everything I could. I tried to find out where he was. I met with tens of lawyers in order to convince them to be our lawyer, so that we could get some news from Gokhan. I encouraged his family to go to the prosecutor's office to file a petition.

I couldn't sleep for days, thinking "Is he being tortured? Is he doing fine?" While I was going through all these, what really mattered was what Gokhan was going through. And I was going to find that out, unfortunately, only after his death.

Many people who witnessed how Gokhan was slowly murdered in custody, did not remain silent after his death. Instead. they spoke up about the murder, loud and clear. One of the witnesses was the Forensic Medicine Specialist Gurol Berber, who was one of the detainees sharing the same cell with Gokhan. After he was released from prison, he talked to the journalist Ece Sevim Ozturk and told the bitter truth in detail:

It was around 8 am in the morning of Sunday, July 24 when Gokhan Acıkkollu was brought to the cell that I was staying with another detainee called Hasan. He was frightened and traumatized.

The Life and Legacy of Gokhan Acikkollu

We wondered what happened to him. When he pulled himself together after a while, he told us that police came to his house in the previous night and beat him severely. He said it was fortunate that his wife and children were not at home during that time. He was then brought to the Vatan Police Station and tortured for 9 consecutive hours.

He was covered all over with bruises and was psychologically broken. He was swaying back and forth nonstop, and shutting himself off. Although we tried to calm him down, he was constantly shaking and rocking. Apparently, he had been taken to the famous "fourth floor" in the police building, where he was tortured and interrogated in one of the torture rooms for nine hours.

While comforting Gokhan that day, I said, "Don't worry, they won't mess with you anymore." I was hoping so because I thought that if they tortured an ordinary teacher for 9 hours nonstop and they couldn't get anything important from him, they must have realized that Gokhan didn't know anything.

They didn't take Gokhan to the doctor for two days. When he finally had a chance to see a doctor, Gokhan told him what he had been through, or rather what they did to him, and the doctor recorded them all. The doctor even took the photographs of the torture marks on his body. This is what Gokhan told us after he came back to the cell.

In the following days, they brought two more people into our cell which was designed for only two people to stay. It was so crowded inside that it was impossible to sleep without putting your foot on someone else's face. They did not give proper food or water to drink. But the worst thing was that almost every night they were coming and taking one of us away to interrogate. We were so helpless and there was nothing that we could do to prevent this.

On the fifth night of his detention, they came and took Gokhan again for interrogation and torture. We helplessly watched him leave, and prayed for him. It was all we could do. When he was brought back five hours later, he was again devastated. This time, they had hit him especially on the back with their knees - many times - and he was really hurting. He was constantly holding his chest and his legs with his hands. When our cellmate Emrah (the lawyer Engin Emrah Bicer who was staying in the same cell as a detainee) went next to him and gently hugged him for support, Gokhan leaned on his chest and cried for several minutes. None of us could say anything. In such a situation there were no words to say.

We learned about what happened when he calmed down a little. Apparently, as soon as he walked in through the door of that room, one of the police officers had yelled at him, "Why are you looking at my face, huh?" and began kicking and punching him. When Gokhan averted his eyes, they beat him again, this time yelling "Why don't you look at my eyes?!" He was beaten and insulted for five hours. "You are a traitor! It's all because of you!" In the following days, Gokhan had frequent nervous breakdowns and diabetic comas. He was being murdered, in a slow motion."

The Life and Legacy of Gokhan Acikkollu

Another person who was in custody in the same cell with Gokhan was contacted by the *Stockholm Center for Freedom*[27] through his lawyer, and he revealed important facts about the custody process of Gokhan that led to his death. His description of what happened supported the statement given by Gurol Berber. He said that he stayed in the same cell with Gokhan for 14 days:

"When he was first brought in, he had beat marks, bruises, and scratches all over his body. During our detention, they took him three or four times, beat him, and brought him back after several hours. For the first four or five days, medical checks were done by doctors on duty in the Forensic Medicine Institute. Later on, the general practitioners or assistant doctors who were working at the hospital came for the medical checks. During the initial medical checks, Gokhan told the doctors about everything he was going through, and the doctors recorded it. He once told us that he asked the doctors to take photographs as evidence, and they did. However, he said that when he was referred to other doctors, the police officers on duty ridiculed him, saying, "Would you like to have a city tour, as well?"

Since he was having unexpected panic attacks, he started to shut himself off from the outer world. He was usually shaking,

---

27 Stockholm Center for Freedom (SCF) is a non-profit advocacy organization that promotes the rule of law, democracy and human rights with a special focus on Turkey. SCF was set up by a group of journalists who have been forced to live in self-exile in Sweden against the backdrop of a massive crackdown on press freedom in Turkey.

uncontrollably. Once he leaned on the shoulder of a detained lawyer named Emrah (Engin Emrah Bicer) and cried for several minutes. He was being handcuffed while taken to the medical checks. Because of this, a few times he did not even want to go to the checkups. One of our cellmates once said that he saw Gokhan being dragged in the hallway and beaten meanwhile. On one occasion, after he was severely beaten by the police, they deliberately skipped the next medical check."

Later on, after the cause of death was officially recorded as "torture" by forensic medicine specialists, *Stockholm Center for Freedom* prepared a 68-page report about Gokhan titled "Tortured to Death"[28] which included the statements of the witnesses, medical reports, and other evidence obtained. In the report, the names of the police officers on duty during the detention period of Gokhan were openly mentioned, demanding compliance with the "Principles on the Effective Investigation and Documentation of Torture and Other Cruel, Inhuman or Degrading Treatment or Punishment"[29] set by the UN General Assembly.

---

[28] https://usercontent.one/wp/stockholmcf.org/wp-content/uploads/2017/11/Tortured-to-death-holding-gokhan-acikkollus-killers-to-account_report_21.11.2017.pdf?media=1643837595

[29] https://www.ohchr.org/en/instruments-mechanisms/instruments/principles-effective-investigation-and-documentation-torture-and

The Life and Legacy of Gokhan Acikkollu

GUROL BERBER'S ACCOUNT OF GOKHAN'S LAST NIGHT

"Although we had been detained for 13 days, Gokhan's statement had not even been taken yet. Since we were brought in a few days before him, we had a court hearing scheduled for the next day, and we would be either released or arrested and sent into a prison, So, this way or that way, that night would be our last night we would spend together with Gokhan. During our time together, we had given him constant moral support, so he was stressed out about our departure. He expressed his sadness that day, saying 'You are leaving, I will be all alone here.' But unfortunately, he would leave our cell before we did.

Gokhan just couldn't stay in small and enclosed spaces, he was getting very nervous. Since the day he was brought to the cell, he once had a diabetic coma and another time a panic attack. Of course, this is only what we had witnessed; we didn't know what was happening when he was taken away for torture.

For 13 days, we had shared our grief and sorrow together. Some days we were making plans about the near future. When we get out, we would write a theatre play script about all that we have been living through in this cell. We were just trying to make the situation a little better, by daydreaming. Gokhan loved the idea of writing a play script and he was very enthusiastic about it. But then again, destiny had its own plans, which was different than our plans.

Seeking justice, by any means necessary…

August 5, 2016…Vatan Police Headquarters, Detention Cell C-3.

That day they took Gokhan from the cell again and brought him back in the evening, devastated. He must have been in severe pain because he was constantly holding his chest. When it was late in the night, it was only both of us who were still awake in the cell. Five of us were staying in the small cell which was designed for only two. It was very hot and stuffy inside and I couldn't sleep. When Gokhan turned towards me in pain and pointed the right side of his chest, all I could say was: "Try to sleep." He turned left and right for quite some time and finally fell asleep. Soon after, I did, too.

After a while, I woke up to noises and saw that Gokhan was writhing in agony, unconscious. Other cellmates had surrounded him, meanwhile shouting for help in desperation. Finally, a few police officers came running. While they were carrying him in their arms, I saw his head tilting back and shouted 'Hold his head! Hold his head!' After a few seconds of uncertainty, I decided to follow them. I thought he was going into a diabetic coma or having a nervous breakdown like before, and I told the police officers to bring some sugar.

Forensic medicine expert doctors Haluk Ince and Lokman Basar were staying in the adjacent cells. Police asked them to help. While I was trying to put some sugar in his mouth, Dr. Lokman checked his pulse. He had none! The two doctors performed CPR for several minutes, and after a while Dr. Haluk said, "We lost him." Afterward, when the ambulance came, they took us back into our cells...

I was very worried about his condition. After a while, one of the officers came by, and I looked at him with a hope he'd say "he is fine" but he didn't. Instead, he lowered his head and averted his eyes, I realized that we had lost Gokhan!

As a cellmate of him, I can say that 'Gokhan Acıkkollu was tortured to death.' As a Forensic Medicine Specialist, I can say that Gokhan Acıkkollu was not only systematically beaten and physically tortured, but he was exposed to serious psychological torture, too. During his time in the cell, he kept saying, "My brother is also a police officer, we are people who serve their country and nation. I don't deserve these cruel treatments!" We had observed a few times how lively and vibrant personality he had, when he was able to take his medication. But all that physical and mental torture just devastated him. Since he was a panic disorder patient, he couldn't easily get over in his mind with all that he was going through. During the night, his mind was making him experience the same things over and over again. We knew that his blood sugar levels had dropped a few times during his torture sessions. If that had happened during the torture on his last day and if he was not given some sugar, this could have triggered the heart attack."

Seeking justice, by any means necessary...

The statement of another detainee who was staying in the adjacent cell on the night of Gokhan's death, was confirming Gurol Berber: *"There was a stirring in the next cell in the middle of the night. The police came to our cell and took a detained doctor out to help them. When he came back after a while, his hands were trembling and he could hardly say: "We lost him." Gokhan had died. According to the doctor, there were signs of beating and torture on his head and body. Perhaps his heart could not bear the torture anymore. 'He died of a heart attack,' the doctor said. This was because Gokhan was subjected to severe torture that day and was brought back to the cell in the evening, crawling between two policemen."*

"MAY I NEVER BE RELAXED IN THIS WORLD!"

I was following every step meticulously. I often called the corresponding police division and asked whether the file had been sent to the prosecutor's office or not. When I finally learned that it was sent, I called my lawyer and let him know, and then asked my brother to go to the prosecutor's office and get a copy of the file.

In the file we received from the prosecutor's office, there were video recordings[30] of the detention cell regarding the moments of Gokhan's death. I couldn't

---

30 https://www.youtube.com/watch?v=MPKQEDUdjnI

watch that video recording for a long time. I simply could not find that courage in myself. But I read the transcript in the file and took detailed notes. I studied it for days and underlined the key passages. On his last night, when he had realized that his condition was getting worse, he shouted for help many times, but the police had not responded to him. So, he was literally left to die. I remember the notes I took as if it was only yesterday: "Why isn't there a police officer on duty in the hallway? How can the officer in front of the security surveillance monitor not notice the help cries of someone who is about to die?"

I kept the video footage of Gokhan's death for three years and didn't have the courage to watch it. Then I gave it to *BOLD* Media and they published the video on their social media. Yes, it was too late for my husband, and there was nothing that could be done, but I could perhaps save the lives of some other people who were staying in the prisons or detention centers and being tortured. So many arrested people had lost their lives in prisons and they had not even been to court yet. Some people had told me, "The government takes good care of its citizens, even of those who are in prisons. Torture in this day and age? Nonsense! If he is innocent, he will be acquitted eventually!" I wanted those people to read what was happening in this day and age! What happened was

Seeking justice, by any means necessary...

a product of a cruel oppression! We had lost our loved one and I wanted those responsible to be punished. It wasn't vengeance that I wanted. How could that bring the man I loved back to me, anyhow? Besides, what possible punishment of those perpetrators could actually bring peace to my heart in this world? Even if they were convicted and punished, I wouldn't feel relieved. My sole purpose was that whoever had persecuted us should not continue to live comfortably. When they were to persecute others, they should stop for a moment and think about the heavy price they will pay for their actions.

That video footage, published in *BOLD* Media, deeply affected anyone who had any remnant of a conscience left in their hearts. And after three years, I finally found some courage for the first time to watch the video on the website of *BOLD* Media. Again and again and again! I've witnessed the last moments of the man I've loved, his writhing movements, and his calls for help. For days, I couldn't get over with what I saw in the video. So many questions were bombarding my mind like: "What was he thinking right there? What was he feeling at that moment? Oh, how much he is in pain! How can they still say there is no torture? Why was there no police around? The man is dying, why is no one helping?! Could he survive if they had come to help earlier?" Of course, I am not questioning God's Divine Decree and Destiny, but only if that police officer who was supposed to be on duty in that hallway that night would indeed have been there! At least, if only the officer who was supposed to be in front of the security surveillance monitor would have been where he was supposed to be! I just couldn't help thinking "If only…, if only!" Sometimes I was getting sad, thinking "Did he feel a lot of pain during the dying process?" Yet, some other times I was consoling myself by thinking "It actually didn't take too long for him to surrender his life." Then I would think of his cellmates and feel sorry for them. Who knows how traumatic this must have been for them!

Seeking justice, by any means necessary...

Photos showing the last moments of Gokhan Acikkollu

https://www.youtube.com/watch?v=MPKQEDUdjnI

04: 26 am Standing in front of the iron bars and shouting to police for help.

04: 35 am The moment of the heart attack

04:36 am Showing no life symptoms

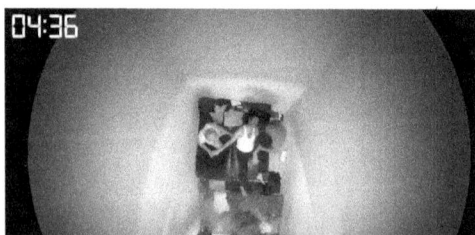

All that matters for me is that one day when justice comes, those perpetrators will receive the punishment they deserve and those family members of the victims will have a piece of relief. And those who oppressed innocent people will have their courage and arrogance broken. When the stories of the oppression are told loud enough for the entire world to hear it, perhaps there wouldn't be any new government plots like the one of "July 15" and there wouldn't be new victims. That is my only hope.

Otherwise, if the troubles that the oppressors will have in this world will lessen their punishment in the Hereafter, I want them to live here with full comfort. Let them enjoy this world! Let my heart find no comfort in this world! That's all right. Because I know that there is a Hereafter. I know that those oppressors will face the eternal justice and punishment there.

They very well know how wrong and corrupted they are. On the other hand, we know that we are on the right side and we are so grateful and humble for that. And that realization alone is sufficient. Yes, they live in their palaces in this world. Suffering from extreme paranoia, they spend each night in a different one of those thousand rooms in their palaces for security reasons, yet they will never attain the tranquility we carry in our hearts! All Praise be to God!

Seeking justice, by any means necessary...

There is one more thing I would like to put on record here...which, I hope, will testify in the Hereafter when I meet my Lord. If I were given a choice today, if I were to be offered that I will be able to go back to my life before July 15, 2006...that I will live happily for a lifetime with my husband, children, and friends...but in return I will give up my relationship with *Hizmet*!

Would I do that? Well, here is my answer.

May the entire world hear it and may God be my witness that I would NEVER accept that offer! I would never give up Hizmet, never!

We have not done anything wrong, neither against God, nor against the people.

We don't care how we are treated in this world! They might as well torture us!

We will be of those who are patient! We will expect our reward from God and God alone!

WITNESSES TO THE FACT THAT GOKHAN ACIKKOLLU WAS TORTURED TO DEATH

When I learned that the file was sent to the prosecutor's office, I called my brother who was at work and asked him to go and get a copy of it. He was kind enough to get it.

But then he returned to his work, and I just couldn't wait patiently until the evening since I was very curious about what was in it. I called him immediately and asked, "Did you look at the file, yet?" He said "Not yet." I insisted, "Please have a look at it. Who put the complaint against Gokhan? Who slandered him?" We hadn't known that until that day. My brother opened the file and read his name to me! It was such a shock to me! I didn't believe what he said. How could this be? It was the name of the person whom my husband trusted so much, he often said, "I doubt myself, but I never doubt him." It was that same person who was arrested before Gokhan, and on the way from Konya to Istanbul, Gokhan was making plans of hiring a lawyer for him, and helping his family members. I asked my brother again and again whether he was sure. My brother read the corresponding line exactly to me: "With the sincere confessions of so and so…" That is why my husband had been taken into custody. I still could not believe it, my brother took a photo of the page and sent it to me.

Was I angry? No, I was not angry, but I was very disappointed. As a matter of fact, I have to say that the same person had later retracted his statement during his first court hearing, saying that he had given that statement under torture and threat. Who knows, they might have threatened him with his wife and his children and forced him to slander innocent people.

I was spending my days working on every small detail in my husband's case file, just like a lawyer. There were many inconsistencies in the file. While the date of his arrest was stated as July 23 somewhere, it was referred to as July 24 on another page. There were discrepancies regarding the time and place of his death. While it was written in some parts of the file that "CPR performed at Haseki Hospital, death occurred at 6:15 am in the morning," the statements of paramedic emergency doctors and employees who had responded to the situation in the police building were contradicting that. According to the emergency medical technicians who performed CPR in the police building, "*The resuscitation efforts did not yield any results. Despite CPR, the person did not make it. When we arrived, he was already dead.*" Moreover, Dr. Haluk Ince, who was detained in the adjacent cell and upon the request of the police, had performed the very first CPR, stated that my husband "passed away in his cell."

We did not make such a request from anyone, but a few people who were detained together with Gokhan and witnessed all the torture submitted their written testimonies through their lawyers and added their names into the list of witnesses in our court case. One of these individuals was a detained lawyer, Engin Emrah Bicer, whom I have already mentioned above. In his handwritten statement to the prosecutor's office on September 20, 2016, following the death of my husband, he wrote: *"While I was in detention, I stayed for 14 days in the same cell with the teacher Gokhan Acikkollu, who was detained due to another investigation. He was beaten to death while he was in custody. This is a fact and at least 15 people are witnesses of this fact. The evidence is solid. I respectfully request that you let me know whether an investigation has already been launched about his death and if so, I request that you provide me with the investigation number."*

Seeking justice, by any means necessary...

Petition sent by Engin Emrah Biçer to the Prosecutor's Office

September 20, 2016

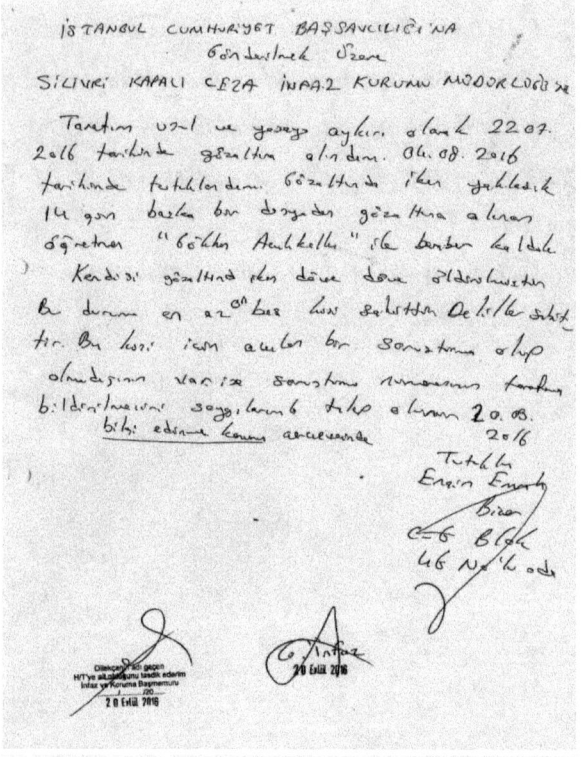

Also, forensic medicine specialist Gurol Berber (who was later imprisoned in Silivri) reached us through his lawyer and informed us that he wanted to testify. Yet another witness, who was an arrested journalist, said that he wanted to testify about how Gokhan was murdered slowly. Other than these, several other detainees, including journalists, doctors, soldiers, and theologians also testified similarly. Neither Gokhan nor I knew these people before, but they wrote and sent their statements of their own free will, even though we did not make such a request from any of them.

According to the testimonies of other witnesses, the day before his death, Gokhan could not stand the torture anymore and shouted "I can't take it anymore! I'm ready to sign whatever you want from me!" But when he was asked to give names, to slander some innocent people so they can get arrested, he had refused.

Again, as far as we have learned from the witnesses, on August 3 he was taken from his cell to the torture room and when his situation got serious, he was immediately brought to the Haseki Hospital where he stayed under medical observation for four hours. But there he was forced to sign a paper saying, *"My name is Gokhan Acikkollu and I do not want to be seen by a doctor."* Do you really think that a person with health problems, after being exposed to severe torture, would have voluntarily said that he "doesn't want to see a doctor?" If for nothing else, he would want to be seen by a doctor, just to stop the ongoing torture. Besides, every time he was taken to a doctor, this person stated that he was being tortured.

Seeking justice, by any means necessary...

He was telling the doctors that they hit his head on the concrete walls many times, and he had been slapped in his face hundreds of times. He was showing the marks of torture on his neck. Again, according to what we have learned from the statements of the witnesses, he got kicked in the ribs several times on July 26 and said that the pain in that area was just unbearable for several days. Indeed, later in the autopsy report, it was stated that there were fractures in his ribs.

In addition, the ridiculous statements in the report of the Forensic Medicine Institute's Board of Experts about the fractures in Gokhan's ribs indicating that *"The fractures happened during CPR"* were easily refuted by the expert doctors. Because the fracture in Gokhan's ribs was close to the abdominal cavity, not to the heart, hence it was medically impossible to break his ribs in that area while performing CPR.

Haseki Teaching and Research Hospital
General Forensic Examination Form
August 3, 2016

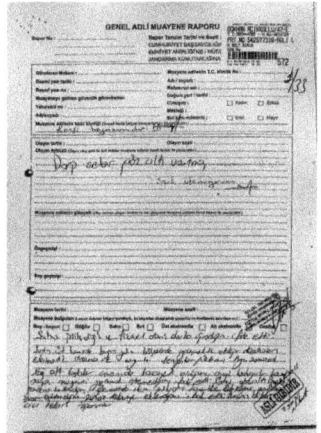
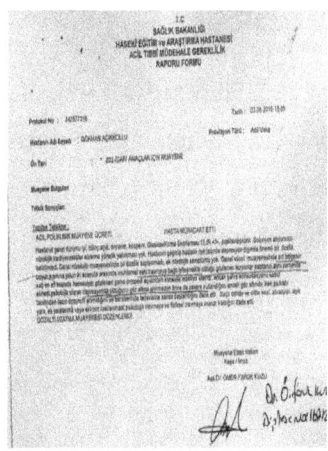

"*The patient states that he was exposed to psychological trauma and physical trauma; his general condition is good and he is conscious; there is no condition in the patient history except depression. There were no additional neurological symptoms in the general neurological examination. Between the two scapulae near the neck in the back region the patient was diagnosed with convalescent lesions, (possibly due to a previous trauma), and at the same time he was diagnosed with lower right posterior tenderness. An orthopedic examination was recommended, but he did not agree to the consultation. Psychologically depressed, took Paxera before being detained; however, the dose was increased by psychiatry when he was in custody, along with*

Seeking justice, by any means necessary...

initiating the use of Xanax. There is no open wound, cut, abrasion or ecchymosis on the scalp."

I had sent Gokhan's medicines to the police station, but after his death they had returned the medicine bottles back to me, and almost exactly with the same amount of medicine inside the bottles. All in all, my husband was murdered by torture and because his medicines were not given to him. No statutory limitation applies to the prosecution of the crime of torture. Those people who are responsible for the death of my husband will eventually be held accountable, first in front of the common conscience and then before the law.

NO NEED TO PROSECUTE!

For the next entire month, we waited for autopsy reports to come out. Immediately afterward, without wasting any time, Prosecutor Burhan Gorgulu decided that there was no need for prosecution. It was an irrefutable fact that my husband Gokhan was murdered, we had provided all the evidence to the prosecutor's office. Yet Mr. Gorgulu had given the decision of no prosecution, in a flash.

The Life and Legacy of Gokhan Acikkollu

Decision of non-prosecution

December 20, 2016

Burhan Gorgulu, Prosecutor of Istanbul

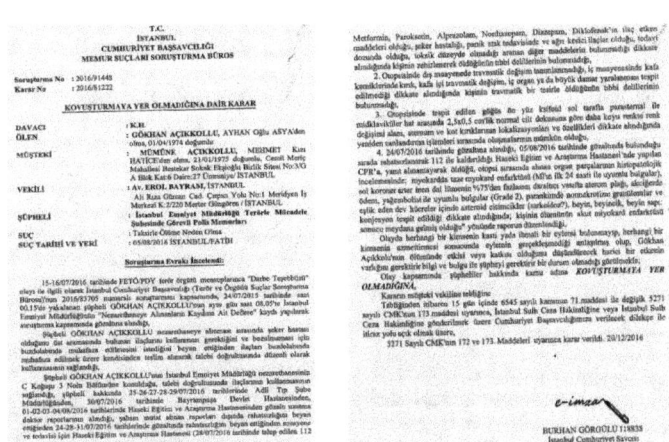

Plaintiff: *Mumine Acikkollu*

Suspect: *Police officers in the Istanbul Counter-Terrorism Police Branch*

In the death of Gokhan Acikkollu, no one has an intentional or negligent act, and no accomplice is present, either. There is no reason to doubt that there is an external factor in the death of Gokhan Acikkollu for there is no clear evidence for any factor. Hence it is decided that there is no reason for any prosecution of the suspects.

The case was getting closed without even taking

the testimony of any witnesses, especially of the lawyer Emrah Bicer, who was added in the investigation file after he had sent a statement to the prosecutor's office. Much later, I would figure out the inside story when I spent some time on the social media accounts of that prosecutor. Apparently, he was a staunch supporter of the ruling party AKP who has used the judicial system to cringe to the executive branch of the government, has become a puppet of the daily politics, and who didn't mind to do anything to butter up the politicians and getting directives and orders from them.

We were left helpless after the decision of non-prosecution. Actually, during that time, a law had already been enacted by a government decree to exempt the police and other security officers involved in the fight against terrorism from any prosecution related to their conducts and activities. We filed a compensation lawsuit against the Ministry of Internal Affairs, but a decision of non-jurisdiction was taken quickly. Then we appealed to the Criminal Court of Peace.

While all this was going on, I was getting many interview offers, of course mostly from the foreign press. Since most of the Turkish media was pro-government this way or that way, no one was eager to see our case objectively and dig for the truth. I told my lawyer Erol

Bayram several times to accept these interview offers and let the public know about what had happened, but he thought that we should wait. He said, "If they try to cover up the case, then we will share it with the media and perhaps then our appeal will be accepted in the Court of Peace." Media attention could change the course of the case. Around that time, Prosecutor Gorgulu had given the non-prosecution decision hastily.

Was there anything else I could possibly do to make my voice heard? Pretty much no, nothing. Not too much time had passed since the so-called July 15 coup attempt and the general atmosphere was incredibly tense. You could neither go out to the streets to demand justice nor was there any platform where you could make your voice heard. Although I gave a few interviews to the foreign media, it didn't make much impact because of the lack of courage and interest of the local media. As a matter of fact, due to the overly delicate situation Turkey was in at that time, no one dared to express any argument against the government even on social media, let alone on the traditional media. So pretty much there was no way we could bring the murder of my husband to public attention. If a person would criticize the government openly in street, he would be arrested and nobody would know when he would be seen again. State of emergency

Seeking justice, by any means necessary...

had just been declared, they were arresting anyone who had the courage to speak out against the government. Nowadays, the victims of the government decree-laws and the mothers of the arrested military cadets are trying to organize some peaceful campaigns, to some extent. But back then, it was absolutely impossible. So, I couldn't do anything else.

I also had to take care of my children. Their father had already been killed, and they couldn't stand to lose their mother now. In any case, it has not been in our Hizmet culture to this day to go out in the streets and demand justice. We were truly people of peace and we have not known anything even about organizing protests. But yet, the government had declared us blood-thirsty murderers! It was impossible to find a journalist in Turkey who had the courage to write about Gokhan's murder. A couple of pro-government journalists reported on it, but their news was full of lies and slanders such as, *"FETO is just using propaganda and agitation, but Gokhan Acıkkollu was the imam and shadow head of the police department, he gave the order for the military coup!"*

The Life and Legacy of Gokhan Acikkollu

Sabah Daily Newspaper March 1, 2018

Another black propaganda of FETO collapsed!

He [Gokhan Acikkollu] was a secret leader and ByLock user!

Takvim Daily Newspaper March 1, 2018

Another black propaganda of FETO collapsed! He [Gokhan Acikkollu] was a secret leader and ByLock user!

Seeking justice, by any means necessary...

Although we could not make our voice heard within Turkey, news and interviews about our case made a significant impact abroad. In France, for instance, public awareness had been raised after these news came out, and many of our friends were given permanent residency much easily. Unfortunately, human rights violations in Turkey were receiving some public attention only in countries where the rule of law was strong, and nowhere else.

Even though prosecutor Gorgulu had quickly closed our case, I was not going to give up. Sebnem Gorur Fincanci, MD, a forensic medicine specialist and the president of the Turkish Medical Association as well as the president of the Human Rights Foundation of Turkey at that time, wrote an article about my husband after his death. In her article, she stated that "neither the Istanbul Protocol nor the Minnesota Protocol had been complied with" regarding the case of Gokhan. She had pretty much shouted to the world that the king was naked, and doing that then was - and still is - a truly brave move. The Istanbul Protocol outlines how the medical checks should be conducted while a person is in detention or incarceration, while the Minnesota Protocol outlines how an autopsy should be conducted after a potentially unlawful death of a person while he was in detention or incarceration. Turkey had signed these protocols. After Dr. Fincanci's article, I read both protocols many times and took notes regarding which rights of Gokhan were violated while he was detained.

THE ARTICLE OF SEBNEM GORUR FINCANCI, MD

"…I had already spent the week beside myself with anger. My dear comrade Celalettin Can and my dear colleague Onur Hamzaoglu, the honorable member of our profession were recently arrested. Dear Onur had shared the pathetic state of the detention conditions and medical checks. And now, on top of all that, the Istanbul Chief Public Prosecutor made a statement regarding the death of the teacher Gokhan Acıkkollu who died in custody right after the coup attempt as a result of torture, claiming that "all allegations that he died as a result of torture are for organizational propaganda purposes and do not reflect the truth."

Even though the high criminal court's contrived reasoning is ironically chilling, it is equally appalling that the prosecutor's office ignores the medical evidence and says that the torture allegations do not reflect the truth, by calling it "organizational propaganda." Of course, this is not the first time that we have seen this type of discourse. More than twenty years ago, a Minister of Justice had the nerve to ask me whether I was a supporter of the Revolutionary

Seeking justice, by any means necessary...

People's Liberation Party about a report that I wrote. Furthermore, one of the mayors of this city had declared me an enemy of the state and denied the "so-called torture" because I had written that a person died from torture based on the findings of the autopsy. Similar statements and approaches with repetitive features are the main reasons for the existence and continuation of torture in this country.

However, we ordinary citizens also have an important responsibility in the continuation of torture. Gokhan Acıkkollu died in August 2016, his family had called upon the Human Rights Foundation of Turkey to get a second opinion about the causes of his death, since his family did not feel like they had been given justice after the autopsy report was released. It wasn't until January 2017 that the medical evaluation of the Human Rights Foundation of Turkey was completed. During this period, allegations of "torture" came to the forefront, albeit in a low voice, and many violations, including the shame of his attempted burial in a "traitor's cemetery" took place, but the public didn't care.

At the beginning of 2017, the relationship between his death and torture was shown and shared as a result of the medical evaluation, but that didn't get the attention of the public for the entire year of 2017. One and a half years after his death, a note has been shared in the media stating that he had been reinstated to his job by the government, and only then people began to discuss the "torture of an innocent person."

The Life and Legacy of Gokhan Acikkollu

While the Office of the Chief Prosecutor and the authorities, with speed and determination, denied the claim that he had died as a result of torture, that speed and determination was not present during the investigation of the torture allegations. The only thing that they were in a hurry to prove was his crime. In their minds, if he is guilty, torture is justified, and those who say he died from torture are spouting organizational propaganda.

This is where the responsibility of the ordinary citizen begins. The public must strongly defend the rule that no one can be tortured regardless of who he is, whether he has committed a crime or what kind of crime he has committed. Because citizens should know that in a country where torture is legalized, no one is safe and far from torture. The medical doctors who are citizens of this country should refuse to conduct their examinations in detention facilities. It is imperative that they perform a comprehensive and holistic examination of the detained, including their mental status.

I always think that we physicians have a unique and valuable privilege. Even in war, our medical obligation to treat the enemy soldier requires us to be free from the burdens imposed on us by this world. Human rights advocacy should be a natural consequence of being a medical doctor, and for that reason, it is necessary to investigate whether torture was done, regardless of to whom it was done."

Seeking justice, by any means necessary...

THE EMPEROR HAS NO CLOTHES!

We decided to ask Dr. Fincanci for a new and more detailed autopsy report. Before that, my lawyer Erol had done some research and learned that Istanbul University was also able to issue a detailed autopsy report. But frankly, since it is a government institution, it did not give me any confidence. When I learned that the "Human Rights Foundation of Turkey" headed by Dr. Fincanci at that time also had this authority, I did not even think twice about it.

Dr. Fincanci prepared a new autopsy report using the documents and evidence we had collected. I could see it much more clearly now. My husband's murder by the government had taken place in stages. Every time he was taken for a doctor's checkup, he explained his situation and asked for help. Although most of the doctors did not have the courage, some conscientious ones took notes in their reports. We read the following notes in those reports: "He said that he was hit hundreds of times in the face... He was kicked in the ribs... He was hit in the back with knees." The reports also stated that "signs of the rupture of the brain vessels observed in several places on the scalp...he has ecchymoses (bruises) consistent with what he describes..." The autopsy reports also confirmed these: "He had hemorrhage points on his back and under his scalp." In addition, "rib fracture" was also reported.

During the doctor's checkup on July 25, 2016, my husband had mentioned that he was kicked under his right rib and that he was in severe pain. According to what he said, he had been hit repeatedly on the head, face, and back…and on the day he was detained, he had been kicked in his right rib cage and it hurt a lot. The doctor had already noted that there was serious bruising in that area. We also read in the autopsy report that there was a fracture in the rib area, and bleeding focal points had formed on his back and scalp. It was incredibly dramatic! Gokhan's rib had been broken the night he was detained. And for the next 13 days, he was exposed to systematic torture with that broken rib. Not as his wife, but I am saying this as a healthcare professional that this situation is incredibly painful. Normally, the area around the broken rib should be wrapped and the person should lie still, but instead Gokhan was subjected to more torture for days.

Seeking justice, by any means necessary...

Institute of Forensic Medicine Report
July 25, 2016

"Acikkollu said that he was taken into custody on July 23 at around 23:00 and was handcuffed from behind while being battered at the same time. He said he has been suffering from panic attacks and that for this reason he regularly uses medication; however, he couldn't use his medication while in custody. There is ecchymosis on both scapula and on the right shoulder, pain in left arm movement and ecchymotic areas on the left scapula measuring 6x6 cm, on the right scapula measuring 6x8 cm and on the right shoulder measuring 5x4 cm."

Institute of Forensic Medicine Report

July 26, 2016

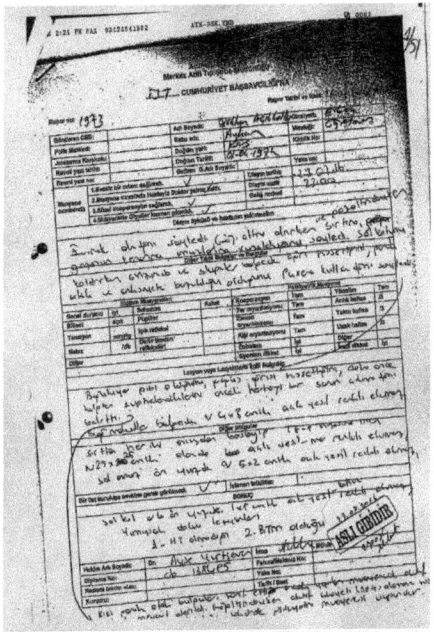

The following statements are from the report that is prepared by a doctor when Acikkollu was taken to the Institute of Forensic Medicine Central Branch Directorate on July 26, 2016.

"He said that while he was taken from his home by police, and then in the custody he was hit on his back, shoulders and eyes. He said that he has pain in the scapular region when he moves his left arm, that he has panic attacks and an anxiety disorder, and that he takes a medication called Paxera. He said that he has chest pain and feels like he is drowning, although much earlier they had checked his heart and no problem was diagnosed. There was light green ecchymosis in the right maxillary region measuring 4x3 cm; green-purple ecchymosis measuring about 25x25 cm, starting on the back of both shoulders and extending to the T8-9 thoracic vertebrae in the torso section of the spine; light green-brown ecchymosis on the middle front left arm measuring 1x5 cm; and light green ecchymosis on the left shoulder measuring 5x2 cm."

The Life and Legacy of Gokhan Acikkollu

Institute of Forensic Medicine Report
July 27, 2016

The following statements are from the report that is prepared by a doctor when Açıkkollu was taken to the Institute of Forensic Medicine Central Branch Directorate on July 27, 2016.

His statements and the doctor's observations as recorded in the report: "*He stated that after yesterday's examination, he was slapped several times on both sides of his face, mostly on the right side; the outside of the right side of his chest was kicked; the back of his head was banged on the wall; and he was heavily sworn at. He is using insulin for type 1 Diabetes (DM) and Paxera for panic attacks. There are green-colored ecchymoses on the right side of his face, on his forehead, around the eyes, under the tragus...contusion along a line of 5 cm, spots of ecchymoses. There is hyperemia in the back side of the head measuring 0.9 cm and pain in the right side of his chest. He states that his panic attacks that are triggered by psychological pressure and he doesn't feel good. Examination is appropriate for the right chest, and psychiatric consultation is appropriate for panic attack disorder."*

Institute of Forensic Medicine Report

July 28, 2016

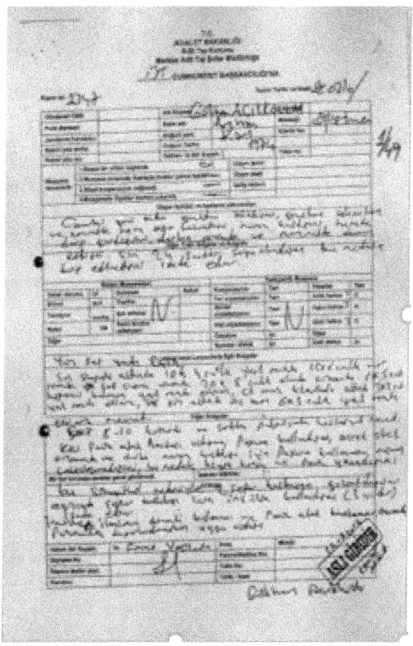

The following statements are from the report that is prepared by a doctor when Acikkollu was taken to the Institute of Forensic Medicine Central Branch Directorate on July 28, 2016.

"He stated that on Saturday he was taken into custody at his home, he was subjected to heavy assault and battery, and this continued in the police car and in the detention room. He has not been interrogated and beaten in the last 24 hours. Swelling is visible

on the right side of the face; there is ecchymosis on the right scapula measuring 10x4 cm, green in color, and measuring 15x6 cm, purple in color; on the right scapula measuring 20x8 cm, green in color with 6x5 cm hyperemia in the middle; on the outside of the right eye measuring 6x5 cm, green in color. There was pain in the back upon palpation, on the right side of the T8 and T10 vertebrae. Patient suffers from panic attacks and is taking Paxera. Since he was subjected to beating; he has not been able to calm down despite the use of Paxera. For these reasons, he experienced great stress and fear. He was taken to the hospital two times due to these complaints, and he has also been taking insulin for diabetes (for 3 years). A policlinic evaluation is appropriate for panic attacks and regular use of insulin is recommended."

The Life and Legacy of Gokhan Acikkollu

Institute of Forensic Medicine Report

July 29, 2016

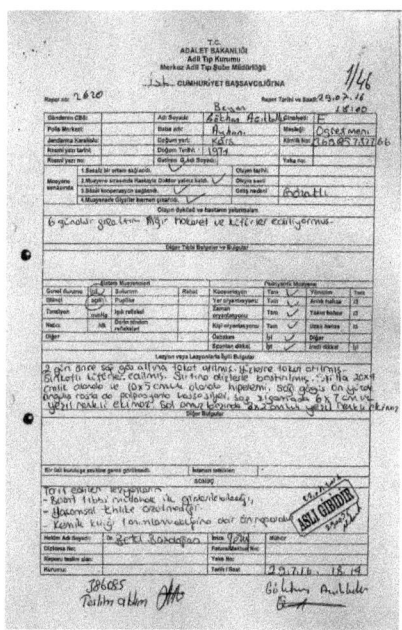

Acikkollu was taken to the Institute of Forensic Medicine Central Branch Directorate on July 29, 2016 again. The following statements are from the report that is prepared by the doctor.

"He said that he was severely assaulted and sworn at during the lasty six days in detention; two days ago his face was slapped under the right eye, slapped hundreds of times. He was subjected to verbal abuse with swearing and insults, and he was hit in the back with knees. There was hyperemia in the back measuring 10x5

Seeking justice, by any means necessary...

cm and 20x4 cm, sensitivity at angulus costae upon palpation, ecchymosis on the right zygoma measuring 6x7 cm, green in color, ecchymosis on the left shoulder measuring 3x2 cm, green in color."

Bayrampasa Public Hospital

General Forensic Investigation Report

July 30, 2016

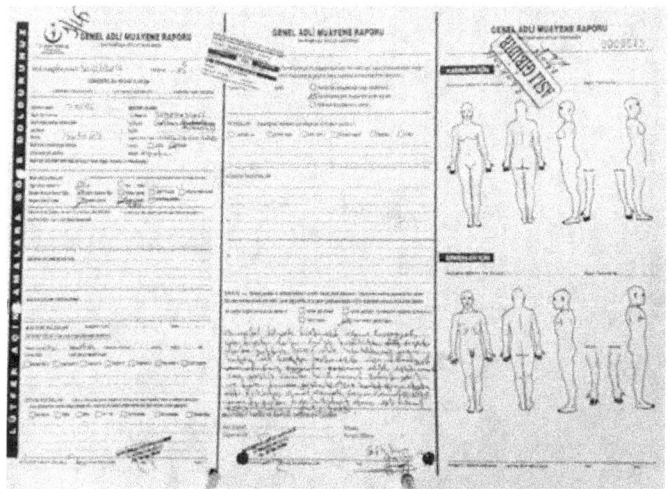

According to the general forensic investigation report from Bayrampaşa State Hospital, *"There is pain and tenderness to the touch in the occipital region; rubescence in the interscapular area measuring 6 cm and in the left scapular area measuring 20x6 cm. There is green and purple swelling on the right side of the zygoma; the right lens of his glasses is broken; and a state of panic and fear was observed. He stated that he had excessive fear. For further screening, he was referred to psychiatry, general surgery, neurosurgery and ENT surgery."*

Seeking justice, by any means necessary...

Istanbul University

Psychiatric Polyclinic Emergency

Mental Health Examination Report

July 31, 2016

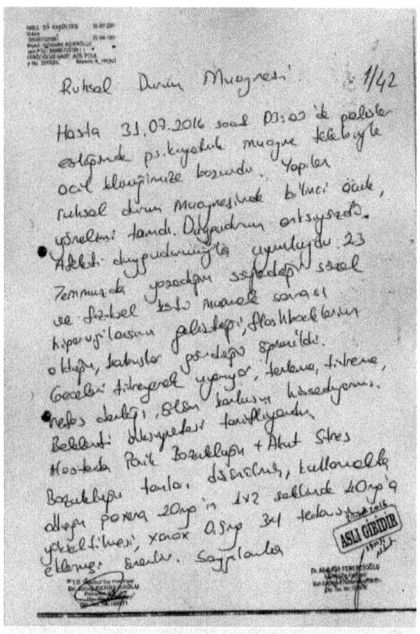

Acikkollu was taken to the Istanbul University – Psychiatric Polyclinic Emergency on July 31, 2016. The following statements are from the report that is prepared by two doctors.

"*Accompanied by police officers, Acikkollu was brought to our Emergency Polyclinic at 3 a.m. on July 31, 2016 for a mental health examination. He was conscious but his mood was anxious and compatible with an affective state and that he had developed hypervigilance after verbal and physical abuse. He has flashbacks and wakes up with nightmares, symptoms of sweating, trembling, shortness of breath, fear of death, anticipation anxiety, panic disorder and acute stress disorder. It is recommended to increase the use of Paxera from 20 mg to 40 mg 1x2 with the addition of Xanax 0.5 mg 3×1."*

Seeking justice, by any means necessary...

Haseki Teaching and Research Hospital
General Forensic Examination Form
August 4, 2016

According to the general forensic investigation report prepared in Haseki Teaching and Research Hospital on August 4, 2016, *"the patient said his right rib cage was kicked; there was pain in his right rib cage; he has DM and panic attacks; he uses insulin, Xanax and Paxera."*

The Life and Legacy of Gokhan Acikkollu

Human Rights Foundation of Turkey

Report of Professor Sebnem Korur Fincanci, MD

January 18, 2017

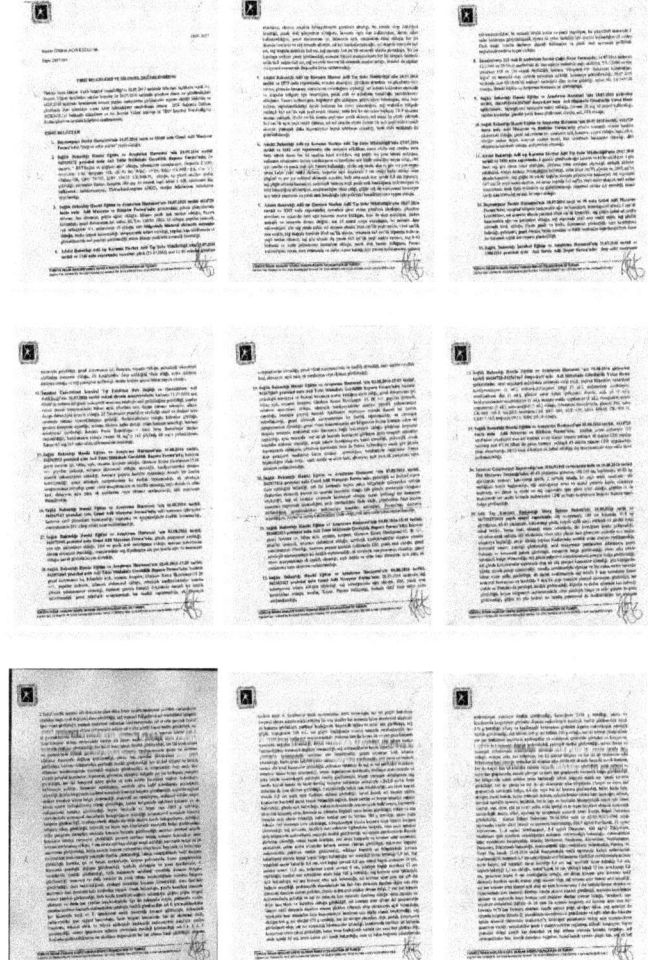

Seeking justice, by any means necessary...

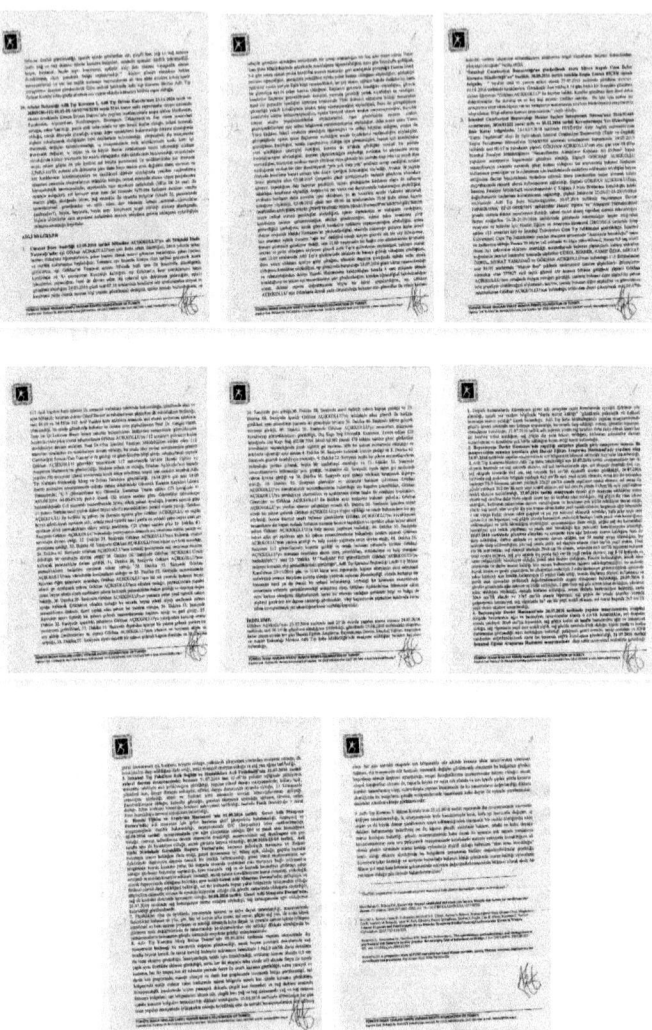

The Life and Legacy of Gokhan Acikkollu

The Conclusion Page of the Report of Professor Sebnem Korur Fincanci, MD

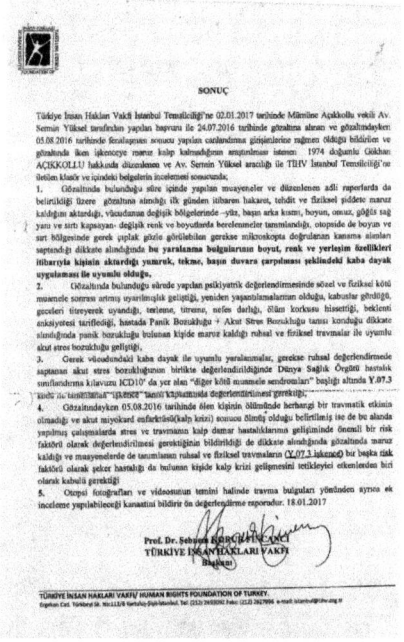

- As stated in the medical examinations and reports during his custody, Açıkkollu complained that beginning from the first day in custody he was subjected to **insults, threats and physical violence**; *bruises of various colors and sizes were found in different parts of his body, such as the face, back of the head, neck, shoulders, right part of the chest, and back; bleeding spaces in the neck and back that can be seen by the naked eye and verified by a microscope are defined in the autopsy. Taking all this into consideration, the findings of injuries in terms of size, color and location are in*

conformity with Açıkkollu's complaints about **rough beating such as punching, kicking, hitting and the banging of his head on the wall**;

- *He had developed* **acute stress disorder**, *which is in parallel with the* **mental and physical trauma** *he suffered;*

- *When the injuries that conform with the definition of* **rough beating and acute stress disorder detected** *in mental evaluations are considered together, the case should be classified as* **torture**, *which can be found under "other ill-treatment syndromes" according to the World Health Organization's ICD-10 International Statistical Classification of Diseases and Related Health Problems.*

- *Although it was stated that he had died of a heart attack, stress and trauma are important risk factors for the development of cardiovascular disease. The* **mental and physical traumas (torture)** *he suffered during his custody which were also detected in the medical examinations should be considered as* **triggering elements of a heart attack** *for a person who also had diabetes as another risk factor.*

Dr. Fincanci wrote in the report, "As a result of all this evidence, it should be recorded that the factor that led to the heart attack was torture." We have added this report to our case file and then appealed to the Criminal Court of Peace again. In our appeal, we stated that our witnesses were not listened to, very few of the camera recordings were given to us, and no information was provided by the police department regarding whether his medications were regularly given and whether he had been provided a diet suitable for diabetics. We added that there was no large-scale investigation conducted and that the case should be reopened.

Prosecutor Burhan Gorgulu had dismissed the case in December 2016. About a month later, in January 2017, we appealed the case to the Criminal Court of Peace. Due to judicial procedure, they had to send us their response within fifteen days, but we waited seven months for it. It was not until July 2017 that our appeal was accepted. Afterward, the lawsuit process finally started, but there would be no progress whatsoever.

During this process, I was in constant contact with our lawyer. The court asked the Forensic Medicine Institute to review the autopsy reports again. They also requested from our lawyer Erol the hospital files with information regarding the medical tests, but they were already in our file that we had sent to them. In short, they were pretty much stalling us.

For the next seven months (until February 2018) there was no progress on the case. It was not until we have received the note about my husband's reinstatement to his job and this caused a public outrage after the news spread on the social media, that the Criminal Court of Peace made a hasty decision: they made the case closed to the public! Afterward, for two years we have not been informed about any development regarding our case, and finally in February 2020 our case has been rejected by the court. Our only option left was to file our case with the Supreme Court. After a short time, I made an individual appeal to the Supreme Court through my lawyer.

I AM BEING DETAINED!

After Gokhan's death, my parents came from Konya to stay with me and my children. During that time my son was in his senior year of high school and was preparing for the university exams. My daughter was enrolled in the school in our neighborhood.

No matter how sad we were, no matter how much we hurt, life had to go on somehow. I could not continue with my job because I was dismissed via decree-law no. 675 on October 29, 2016. The government, which killed my husband while in custody, had also robbed me of my profession, which was my only means of earning my livelihood and supporting my family. We had purchased our apartment using a mortgage loan, and we were making payments every month. I had my son enrolled in a private school, and I was paying his tuition installments. There were of course kitchen and utility expenditures, and many other expenses for my children. I was carrying all the weight on my shoulders.

Well, I was never a person who enjoyed sitting idle. So, I began to make noodles during the day and sell them to friends and acquaintances, and at night I did handworks, knitting sweaters, soft socks for babies, washcloths, and similar items. That is how I was providing for my family. Of course, I can never repay my dear father during this time period. When we were outside for shopping, he would always pay for everything.

Then another door of opportunity opened. Since my husband died before he was dismissed from his job, we had the right to receive a small part of his monthly salary. We applied for it and it was accepted four months later. Thankfully, we were able to breathe a bit easier.

As I mentioned above, while all of this was going on, I was also seeking justice. Even though our appeal was accepted in July 2017, there had been no further development for months, until February 2018. "What happened in February?" you may ask. Well, my husband got reinstated to his job! After the official reinstatement letter arrived and attracted some public attention, the court made a hasty decision and made the case closed to the public.

Before I get into more details, I would like to talk about something that happened about a year before receiving the letter. On February 24, 2017, I was taken into custody!

One day before, on Thursday, I had gone out with one of my friends, and on the way back home we were talking. All of a sudden it came to my mind and I told her: "God has let me live all kinds of pain recently, but not a detention. I sure hope He doesn't let me experience it." That evening my brother came to visit us. My father had been getting a little bored at home lately, and we made plans for the next day. In the morning, my brother would drop us off in Eminonu on his way to work, and we would walk around there for a while and then return by ferry.

The next morning we got up early and got ready. Just as we were about to leave, the doorbell rang. After Gokhan's death, we were getting extra careful and not opening the door immediately. When I looked through the peephole, I saw the security personnel of the housing complex that we were living in. "Can you open please?"

he asked. "Why?" I replied. He asked again: "Can you open it?" I said, "Just tell me what do you want!" Then I noticed the police officers in plain clothes standing at the side. Upon that, I opened the door. My mother, father, brother, and children were all looking at the door in panic.

There they were, a few police officers and next to them the security personnel of the housing complex. "Mumine Tulay Acıkkollu! We have a warrant to search your house and arrest you; we will take you to the police headquarters." I tried to remain calm. "Where is your warrant? Can I see the paperwork?" In response, the officer showed me his police ID. But I wasn't going to give in easily: "You think you can take me with this ID? First, I don't know if this ID is fake. Even if it is real, do you know how many people are taken away by the cops and then disappear for months?"

One of the officers called the police station and spoke to them. After some time, they received an arrest warrant via WhatsApp and they showed it to me. There was nothing regarding the search of the house, they would just take me away with them. While I was going to the bedroom to get dressed, I heard my brother, who is a very kind person, saying to the police officers in all his sincerity: "Wouldn't you like to come in?" I rushed back and said "No! They will wait outside!" I had heard so many stories from my friends about how police was entering into people's homes and planting bug listening devices and false evidence.

After I was dismissed from my job, I had applied to the Court of Appeal and was trying to bring the necessary paperwork together. That day was the deadline for the appeal, and I was going to submit the documents later in the day. Just before I left the house together with the police, I turned back to my brother and said, "Make sure to deliver them today!" That was quite a bold move! The fact that I could think of the deadline of the appeal in such a situation would be the subject of a lot of jokes between us later on, and it would make us smile.

Everyone in the house was looking at me nervously. I told my daughter, "The good police will ask a few questions, I will come back very soon." But to my son I whispered, "Never stop studying for your exams, no matter what happens to me! Take care of each other, these troubles will surely end. Don't do anything that you will regret for the rest of your life!"

My brother followed after us and asked the police where they were going to take me. They would first take me into the Umraniye Police Station to carry out the procedure, and then, if the prosecutor asks for it, I would be taken to the Caglayan Courthouse. My brother made an offer to the cops with his usual kindness: "Can I bring my sister in my car?" I knew my brother very well; if the police had accepted his offer, he would have literally brought me in his car to the police station and handed me over. But of course, the police didn't know that and they said "No, but you can follow us if you want."

I can't say that I was mistreated. First, a pat-down search was made in the Umraniye Police Station. I don't know why it was necessary at that moment, but they took my photos in front of a white cabinet, side-views and front-view. Since it was early in the morning, the police officers inside were having breakfast and chatting at the same time. Of course, the subject of the conversation was us. "You know, when we detain FETO members they give us extra bonuses. Shouldn't we also get rewards when they are eventually arrested?" That was their main concern! Not only they were not showing any kind of remorse, but actually they were expecting bonus and reward because they were very good (!) at depriving poor innocent people of their jobs, homes, and families. I think this scene would be sufficient to summarize the situation that the entire country has been in, recently.

Then one of them, apparently their chief, came towards me and said, "Well, you know your rights." I said

"No, I don't know my rights. It's the first time in my life that I'm dealing with a cop." When I said that, he tensed up a lot. Turning to one of the officers, he said, "Get a copy and give it to her." A police officer stood up and placed a sheet of paper in front of me and then said: "Sign it!" It was supposed to be about detainee rights but at the top of the document it read "Member of PKK[31]". They pretty much asked me to sign a document with someone else's identity information on it! The chief tensed up even more when I said that I would not sign. "Why!?" he yelled in anger. "You say you detained me for being a member of FETO, but there is someone else's name on this paper, and PKK is written all over the place. Are you kidding me or something?" When I said that, they all panicked. They put the document into a shredder right there in front of my eyes and prepared a new one.

Then the police chief told me to take some money with me. "Why?" I asked. "You just take some, all right?" he said. My brother was sitting on the bench in the hallway. I went next to him and said, "They told me to take some money with me." He was also surprised and said, "Why?" I replied, "I don't know, I guess they're going to arrest

---

31 Abbreviation for *Partiya Karkerên Kurdistan* in Kurdish, Kurdistan Workers' Party, which is a Kurdish militant political organization and armed guerrilla movement.

me." I got 50 liras from my brother, but when I went back in, the chief said "That is not enough," so I went out again and asked for some more. I thought, "Probably it will be a very long-term detention, that is why."

Towards noon, I was taken to the Umraniye Research Hospital. They had put something like a counter in a corner inside the hospital, and a doctor was sitting behind it. He didn't check anything, only asked "Have you been exposed to any beating or assault?". When I said "No", he signed a pre-prepared document and handed it to me.

I was then put in a white Doblo van, unmarked. We were heading to the Caglayan Courthouse, and my brother was following us right behind. He also called my other brothers and sisters; they had arrived in Caglayan before us. A female lawyer was working in the office of my lawyer Erol. She had already arrived there, too.

While waiting in front of the prosecutor's office with the police and the lawyer, a thousand feelings and thoughts were running through my mind: "What will the prosecutor ask about? Will he ask me if I had an account in Bank Asya[32]? Whether I visit the houses of my friends

---

32 Tens of thousands of individuals were trialed in "July 15 related" courts, most of them were found guilty and sentenced for imprisonment, for the acts which did not constitute a criminal offense under the law in force at the time it was committed, or even at the time of those trials. Some of those so-called "criminal offenses" were being subscribed to the best-selling

in Hizmet on a regular basis? My children's schools? Would he ask about Gokhan?" I had not entered in the room yet, but I was already feeling tired of thinking about all of these.

At that moment, I remembered a quote from Said Nursi[33]: "*Whenever I am in trouble, a verse of the Qur'an comes to my rescue.*" Waiting there, under extreme stress, I felt that all the reasons had ceased to exist. The prayer of Prophet Yunus (*Jonah*) came onto my tongue first: "*La ilaha illa anta, subhanaka, inni kuntu minaz zalimeen.*"[34] Then, I remembered Prophet Ayyub (*Job*) and said: "*Here I am, in pain, my heart and my tongue are afflicted. But You, my Lord, You are the Most Merciful of those that are merciful!*" I continued: "Oh Lord, please don't let me tell them anything, don't let me betray my sisters and brothers! Don't let me give them the names of innocent people! Let me leave this place in

---

newspaper in Turkey, Zaman, which was in circulation since 1986; having an account in Bank Asya, which was one of the biggest banks in Turkey since 1996; and choosing the schools affiliated with Hizmet Movement for your children to attend. İnviting your friends to your house or visiting them in their houses on a regular basis was also considered a crime.

33 Said Nursi (1876-1960) lived through the decline of the Ottoman Empire, World War I and the emergence of the Turkish Republic. He is one of the most influential Islamic scholars in modern Turkish history. Nursi endured religious oppression and suffered through prolonged periods of exile and imprisonment. His followers reject political ambition, focusing instead on a revival of personal faith through study, self-reform and service of others.

34 Arabic phrase, meaning, "There are none worthy of worship besides You. Glorified are You. Surely I am from the wrongdoers."

peace…and if I can't, please let me not betray anyone!" I kept reciting these prayers so much that after a while, I felt so calm and peaceful. I would find out later that my family was constantly praying for me outside, too.

Just when I was called in by the prosecutor, my lawyer Erol Bayram came running. Erol got permission from the prosecutor to talk to me for five minutes. We went to a corner in the hallway and he asked, "Any idea for why did they detain you?" "I don't know," I replied. "Maybe the bank account, the kids' schools, I don't know." He was quite calm and said, "Well, let's go in and see then!"

I had heard so much about prosecutor Can Tuncay. According to the court records of another arrestee, it was Kayhan Ay, the chief of the Istanbul Counter-Terrorism Branch, who had tortured my husband Gokhan. As a matter of fact, Kayhan Ay had confessed this while he was torturing that other arrestee in the presence of prosecutor Tuncay himself. Journalist Ahmet Donmez had made a news about this, including the corresponding documents and stated the following:

"N.K., one of the defendants in the Istanbul 29th High Criminal Court case related to the activities at the Istanbul Gendarmerie Command on the evening of July 15, gave the name of the then Istanbul Counter-Terrorism Police Branch chief

Seeking justice, by any means necessary...

Kayhan Ay as the perpetrator of the murder of teacher Gokhan Acıkkollu, who was tortured to death while in custody. N.K., in his testimony to the court, explained how Kayhan Ay tortured him: "**During these torture sessions, my blood sugar rose. When I told him that I have severe diabetes, the same person (Kayhan Ay) grabbed my shoulders violently and said, 'Do you remember that teacher who also had diabetes? He died under my hand. I performed his first CPR. Be careful so that you don't end like him. We will keep you here for 30 days.' Then he continued his torture. The prosecutors are witnesses of this torture and threats. Can Tuncay and the other prosecutor were watching and laughing, when Kayhan Ay was torturing me.**" *The person that Kayhan Ay referred to when he said "He died under my hand" was the teacher Gokhan Acıkkollu."*

And yes, now I was in the office of Mr. Tuncay. That was the office where he had used his power and authority to legitimize his unlawful and unjust acts and to butter up the politicians in the government. I knew him only from the media. What I saw when I walked in was a man trying to hide his face behind the files, I could hardly see his face. He never made eye contact with me. I took a quick glance at the papers in front of him and noticed many newspaper clippings from the pro-government media categorized as "evidence."[35]

His first question to me was, "We have looked at your WhatsApp correspondences with your husband. In one of them, he says to you, 'I will talk about this matter to the brother.' Who is this brother?" I have replied: "I have two brothers, and my husband was usually referring them as brothers. Probably he meant them. Besides, you know, we Turks call everyone "brother"… from the taxi driver to the grocery store cashier, even to our school principal, we call brother." My answer did not satisfy him: "You are not helping at all!" he said, displeased. "Sorry, I can't help with what I don't know about," I replied. Then he said, "On the orders of your husband, the soldiers came to the bridge! The blood of 250 people killed that night is on his hands!" At that moment, my heart filled with rage. My husband was not trialed in a court, his statement was not even taken, but now this prosecutor was not only declaring him as a "putschist", but he was also trying to take a statement from me about his crime, which he had never committed. The statement that they wanted to take from him by torturing him. I replied with tears in my eyes, "I hope that the real coup plotters will come to light one day and this slander will be removed from us. But I have

---
[35] Turkish Criminal Law, Article 4 (1) Ignorance of the criminal laws may not be an excuse.

no confidence in this justice system, I trust only in the justice of God. When the real putschists are revealed, I will take them by the scruff of their necks, both in this world and in the Hereafter." He responded by saying, "You're not helping at all, I'm going to arrest you!" The only thing he did afterward was to shuffle the files in front of him while asking questions like, "Who is this brother? Do you know him? Did your husband have any close friend at the Social Services Department?"

He then wrote something on the paper in front of him, turned to me and said in a threatening voice, "Since you are staying with your elderly parents, I'm releasing you for their sake. Otherwise, I would have arrested you!"

When I went out with my lawyer, my older brother came running and hugged me so tight! The big man was sobbing like a child. Right afterward, my sister and brother-in-law, nephew and aunts, and my other brother rushed toward me. Their eyes were red from crying. I would find out later that my younger brother's wife (whom we have recently lost due to a severe illness) had sat on the stairs and read passages from Qur'an in tears, and made everyone cry.

I can't thank my Lord enough. Even though I had lost my husband, at least my family was with me, and we were so close that I was feeling really safe.

When we got out, I thought of the files to be handed over to the Court of Appeal. We told the others to go home, and I went with my brother and handed over the files. It was late afternoon when we got home. My dear mom's and dad's eyes were swollen from crying. Neither they nor my children had eaten anything. They were so happy to see me. It felt like a holiday!

We all had dinner together, and we talked about that stressful day with smiles and laughter. My brother asked, smiling: "For God's sake, tell us what you were thinking while waiting for the prosecutor?" To be honest, this is what crossed my mind for a moment: "Since they told me to get so much money with me, I thought they would surely arrest me. I hoped that they might as well put me in the same ward where the journalist Nazlı Ilıcak was (since I love her very much)!" We all laughed so much when I said that.

We were relieved but still on edge. We did not know what other evil plans they would come up with, how they could further disturb our peace. It was about three days later, my brother brought home a tiny parakeet from a friend who owned a pet shop. He was such a little baby yet that he couldn't even stand on his feet properly. We

Seeking justice, by any means necessary...

named him *Saskin*, (which means in Turkish kind of *silly*, but in a cute way). My kids spent so much time talking to him and they even taught him so many words. This tiny parakeet was so talented that he could eventually recite the prayer of *Subhaneke* (around 10 words), sing the children's song *Mini Bir Kuş (A Tiny Little Bird* – around 20 words*)* and count from one to ten. During those difficult days, that little bird has become such a morale booster for me and my children.

MY HUSBAND REINSTATED TO HIS JOB!

As I mentioned above, Gokhan was reinstated to his job in February 2018, and they had hastily made our court case closed to the public. I would like to explain this in more detail.

The Life and Legacy of Gokhan Acikkollu

Ministry of Education - Umraniye District Branch Reinstatement Letter of Gokhan Acikkollu
February 20, 2018

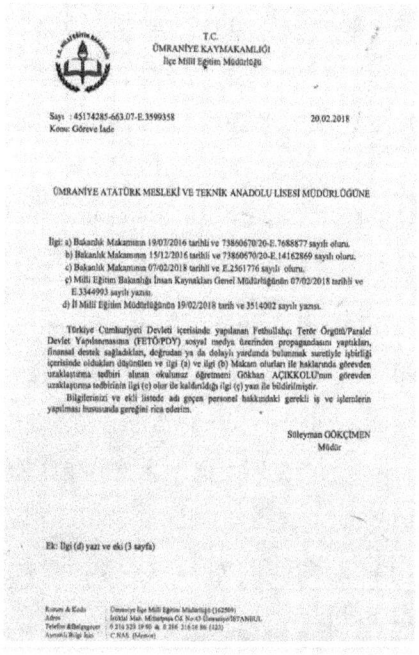

"Gokhan Acikkollu, who had been dismissed from his job as a teacher in the Umraniye Ataturk Vocational and Technical High School, has been reinstated to his job by the notice of the Ministry of Education, dated February 7, 2018."

As far as I remember, it was the 22nd of February. I was out shopping with my son, and I got a call from an unknown number. The voice said that he was calling from Umraniye Ataturk Anatolian Vocational and Technical High School and continued: "Your husband's reinstatement letter has arrived. You have to sign it." I couldn't believe my ears. "Is this a joke? Are you kidding me!?" I responded, "My husband passed away and now he's being reinstated to his job? I'm not signing anything!" He said: "Ma'am, there is nothing I can do about it. Please sign it so that we can send it to the district branch of the Ministry of Education with the cover letter." I said "I will not sign it!" and hung up the phone.

But five minutes later they called again. Apparently, the principal had insisted that the reinstatement letter must be signed and they were asking me again to go to the school and sign it. I lost my temper this time. I said "You can write to your district branch that Gokhan's legal heir is not signing it! Send *that* as a cover letter!" and hung up the phone in his face.

I guess I was just protesting the terrible injustice done to Gokhan with my reaction. But shortly after, it occurred to me that this document could help me in my efforts to prove my husband's innocence. I called back the number and said I'd be there soon.

I went and signed the letter on the condition that I keep a copy. Apparently, the document was sent from the

Ministry of Education to the Istanbul Directorate and then to the District Branch. It was marked with capital letters as "CONFIDENTIAL".

PRO-GOVERNMENT MEDIA TRIGGERMEN TARGETING ME

Journalist Bulent Ceyhan was awarded the prestigious "Metin Goktepe Journalism Award" after making a news about my husband. However, the award was withdrawn later due to the pressure on the jury. Since Bulent had full knowledge of all the details of our case, I decided to send the reinstatement letter to him so that he could report it. After the news appeared on social media, many journalists had contacted me, one after another.

Yavuz Oghan from RS FM called, and we had a productive 15-minute interview on his program *"Bir de Bunu Dinle"* (*And Listen to This*). That interview created a lot of buzz. You know, when someone innocent is arrested or imprisoned, people keep saying, "If he's innocent, he will eventually get out of the jail." I wanted everyone to know that my husband was innocent when he entered into the detention room…and yes, he got out of the jail, but only dead.

Then, Ahmet Hakan from Kanal D covered our

case in his program making a news with the headline "Government Said *Sorry* After 18 Months."

When the news about Gokhan started to appear in the media, Yusuf Tekin, the then Undersecretary of National Education, hastily made a statement saying, "He was not found innocent. We did not reinstate him to his job, we just lifted the administrative measure." I was very upset to hear that. When a reporter from the Turkish BBC News called to talk to me right then, I shared this with him. The reporter took a defensive stance and said: "I often meet with Yusuf while covering education news stories. I know him very well, we are really close. His nature is like that." Well, I didn't like what he said and I didn't want to talk to a news reporter who immediately defends a government official, with whom he is *really close*, without even knowing what we were going through and what kind of person Gokhan was. I politely thanked him and hung up the phone.

While my struggle for justice on behalf of Gokhan continued, the pro-government media did not stay idle. All of them were kind of racing to prove that my husband was a "ferocious terrorist." Suleyman Ozisik from the news portal *Internet Haber* wrote an article with the title, "Look Who Is Innocent Now!" In the article, he did not only target Gokhan but also me and my son.

The Life and Legacy of Gokhan Acikkollu

Then Nazif KARAMAN from the newspaper *Sabah* wrote a slanderous article targeting us. Soon after the Turkish judiciary which was pretty much serving like a hunting dog in the hands of the government puppets took action, and the prosecutor Can Tuncay suddenly decided to prepare an indictment against me. Well, he was surely trying to do his best to fulfill his duty (!) to the ruling party and its government!

I learned about this indictment on March 8, 2018, from the news published in the pro-government newspapers that day. A lawsuit was filed against me demanding a prison sentence of 7 and a half years to 15 years!

Milliyet Daily Newspaper March 7, 2018

Gökhan Açıkkollu'nun eşine FETÖ davası

Fetullahçı Terör Örgütü'nün (FETÖ) 15 Temmuz darbe girişiminin ardından başlatılan soruşturma kapsamında, kalkışmaya iştirak ettiği gerekçesiyle gözaltına alınan ve hayatını kaybeden Gökhan Açıkkollu'nun eşi Mümüne Açıkkollu hakkında "silahlı terör örgütüne üye olmak" suçundan 15 yıla kadar hapis cezası istemiyle dava açıldı.

FETO lawsuit filed for the wife of Gokhan Acikkollu

As part of the investigation started after the July 15 coup attempt of FETO, a lawsuit is filed against Mumine Acikkollu, the wife of Gokhan Acikkollu who was arrested on grounds of

Seeking justice, by any means necessary...

participating in the coup attempt and had later lost his life. 15 years of imprisonment is demanded for Mumine Acikkollu for the crime of being a member of an armed terrorist organization.

Haberturk News Portal March 7, 2018

> **Gözaltında ölen öğretmen Gökhan Açıkkolu'nun eşine FETÖ davası**

FETO lawsuit filed against the wife of Teacher Gokhan Acikkollu, who died under custody.

Yek Vucut News Portal, March 4, 2018

> **"Gökhan Açıkkolu masumdu" propagandası yalan çıktı**

The propaganda of "Gokhan Acikkollu was innocent" refuted.

Turkiye Egitim News Portal March 7, 2018

> **Başsavcılıktan Gökhan Açıkkolu açıklaması**
>
> **TANIK BEYANLARINA GÖRE TANKLARA YOLU AÇIN TALİMATI GÖKHAN AÇIKKOLU TARAFINDAN VERİLMİŞTİR**

Chief prosecutor's office: "Gokhan Acikkollu gave the order to the military tanks to clear the roads.

I immediately called my lawyer. He comforted me by saying that no investigation about me existed in the *UYAP* (National Judicial Network Information System). If it was not in *UYAP*, it meant that there was no lawsuit. As a matter of fact, it was also a crime to inform the media about a case if it didn't exist in *UYAP*.

My lawyer Erol explained all this and told me not to worry, but the truth of the matter was quite different. My lawyer and I became aware of this lawsuit, which did not even show up in *UYAP* system, on March 13th, and only after the indictment was accepted by the 23rd High Criminal Court. A lawsuit was filed against me officially, and the first trial date was set as May 31.

Chapter 6

Even if the wind blows forever,

the mountain never shakes!

A DECIDING MOMENT

I checked the e-government[36] platform and there it was, the lawsuit against me. I called my lawyer and he went to the Caglayan Courthouse to get a copy of the indictment. Honestly, the first thing that came to my mind was: "They're going to arrest me for sure!" Following the media reports about Gokhan's reinstatement to his job, pro-government media had posted many news articles targeting me. I thought these were all a part of the plan to arrest me. And I was afraid that they wouldn't simply stop by arresting me. There were many media news published recently about Gokhan along the lines: "They tortured an innocent person to death and then reinstated him to his job after he died." Since they obviously couldn't arrest Gokhan again and accuse him of something else, they could use me to launch another slander campaign. I was really getting scared of the possibility that they could torture me, too, until I accept to sign a document which states that Gokhan gave the coup order (!) and organized the putschists (!) They would then publish that statement in every news portal across the country. As a matter of fact, even if I refused to sign any document, they could still tell the entire world that I confessed every crime (!) of

---

36 A platform that provides access to government services electronically.

my husband. They had nothing in their hands although they had tortured Gokhan for 13 days. But they could use a statement that they could take from me as a propaganda tool. They could lie and tell the public that I confessed everything.

Well, one might think that these are all nothing but some delusions. But it was as plain as day what could happen in the near future. The only logical thing to do for me was to make a decision. I sat down with my family members and talked to them. I had three alternatives: I could leave my children under the supervision of my parents and move to another place, maybe in another town, to hide. But that was almost impossible for a family like us, since we were really so close to each other. No one in my family could do without seeing me for a long time. The police could easily find me by following them.

My second alternative was to risk everything and eventually go to jail. Well, given that Gokhan was killed in custody, I couldn't just say, "It's all right, eventually I will get out of the jail." My children had already lost their father, I couldn't take the risk of them losing also their mother.

The third and most difficult alternative was to leave this country…the country which pretty much grudged us to stay as a family together! Well, this alternative panicked my family the most. They didn't like the idea and didn't give consent to it. We were hearing about what was happening to those who tried to cross the Turkey-Greece border through the river Maritza. Some drowned in raging waters; some others who could cross the river were detained and then delivered to the authorities in Turkey to get arrested. Yes, some were able to cross the border and build a new life for themselves, but the idea of "What if you can't make it?" was more overwhelming.

My brother said desperately, "Why don't you stay and serve whatever sentence you receive?" I explained to him my concerns: "I'm not afraid of being arrested; I'm afraid of what they might do to me. I can endure being imprisoned unjustly, but I just can't handle all the other things they might do. I just can't!"

A month and a half passed before we could make a decision. I was literally on the horns of a dilemma. I was going through every possible scenario in my mind, again and again. Meanwhile, my son was admitted to the Law School in Istanbul City University with a full scholarship and had already begun his freshman year. What about his education and all his hard work? Okay, let me go to jail, but what if they torture me? What if I can't endure the torture and somehow ruin Gokhan's legacy? What if I

Even if the wind blows forever, the mountain never shakes!

was forced to slander other innocent people?

THE GARBAGE IN THE HEART

I just couldn't make a decision in one way or another, and that uncertainty was really distressing me. I even asked some of my friends, whose character and moral I trusted, to perform *istiharah*[37] for me. I was trying *istiharah*, too, but I was seeing different colors in my dreams and interpreting them differently every single time. What to do? How to decide? I didn't know.

I had serious sleep problems after Gokhan had been detained. If someone were to say something in a little bit loud voice while I was asleep in my room, I would jump up in panic and run towards the house door. Even when we were staying at my brothers' home, I couldn't go to bed without locking the door and putting the bolt on. Once my sister-in-law said, "I get nervous when I wake you up for morning prayers. No matter how quietly I call out your name, you get startled and leap up." I said, "I usually don't sleep in the night until sunrise, no need to wake me up for the morning prayer." Some nights, the

---

37 The istiharah prayer is a special prayer to be performed when an important decision is to be made. After performing the istihara prayer, one typically sleeps and then tries to interpret the things that he has seen in his dream.

housing complex security personnel was walking around with a flashlight in his hand, and when that light hit the window, I would run to the window in panic, "The cops are here!" Even in normal times, I had difficulty in falling asleep, and now it was impossible. I'd forgotten what it was like to have a deep, peaceful sleep without waking up in the middle of the night.

My brothers had a neighbor across the street, a religious old lady, living a simple life. She knew what had happened to my husband, but we never talked about it. I had never told anyone except my immediate family about my plans to go abroad. One day I felt so helpless, and I asked her, without mentioning that I was considering leaving the country: "I can't make a decision about an important matter. Would you please perform *istiharah* for me?" The next day she said to me: "In my dream, you told me, 'Ma'am, I'm going on a boat trip, but there are three pieces of garbage in the house, so I'm going to take them out and then leave.'" As surprised as I was, I looked deep in my heart and thought about what kind of garbage I carried in my heart. My son's school? Our house and car? The hope of being reinstated to my job?

And I made a decision: I was only going to leave after getting rid of the garbage in my heart. Once I made a decision, I shouldn't have looked back.

Even if the wind blows forever, the mountain never shakes!

There is an old saying, "Even the worst decision is better than indecision." This uncertainty was causing such a stress on me that my family members, especially my mother, were getting so upset seeing me like that. Then, one day my mother said, "I think I know what we should do. I have a feeling that this road trip will go okay. If you stay here, and if you get arrested and locked between those four walls, you won't be able to stand it, and neither will I. Just go and take care of your children! That would be the best!"

My mother was able to say this, and in a quite strong manner, but my poor father couldn't say anything; he just cried nonstop. Even though my mother said "Go", the rest of the family had still not given their consent. But I stood firm in front of them: "We've made up our mind, we're leaving. With or without your support!"

I consulted with my son and daughter, too, of course. I was wondering what they thought of leaving. I told them that we were in a junction and there were three alternative paths that we could take. They strongly opposed the idea of continuing with the status quo and taking the risk of me going into prison: "Our father never came back from prison, and now we would never let you go in prison!"

I was so upset when my daughter said, "Please Mom,

please! Let's go, let's leave this place! I hate this country!" It was hurtful to hear that a child-- my child--hated her country. Even on my most difficult day, I had not taught or imposed my children the feeling of hatred. As a matter of fact, we had not even told my daughter how her father passed away, since she was so young. But she found it out from the media after some time, and one day she stood up in front of me and said, "I know how my father passed away!"

My son was considered an adult at that time, and his thoughts were much more important to me. I told him, "If you would want to stay because of your school, I can understand that. I will not go anywhere without you. If you don't agree to go, I'll stay here together with you and accept whatever happens." But he refused and said, "Let's all go together, Mom." It was an important decision, and I didn't want them to blame me for anything that could happen later. I sorted out all the scenarios one by one without twisting them, without making them look attractive. "There will be many challenges for you in a foreign country. You might regret it. Besides, we're not going to leave in a normal way. The trip will be full of troubles, we'll walk a lot, and then get on a boat. There are a lot of risks…" I saw that my kids were just as determined as I was.

Even if the wind blows forever, the mountain never shakes!

By the way, let me make something clear about my children. I hadn't shared the details with them, especially with my daughter, about how their father was killed. But I didn't want to cut them off from any news or developments about their father's death or about what all the other innocent people in Hizmet were going through. My logic was that if they would go through that pain, let's live it all together, because if they were to find out the truth much later, it would be a lot harder for them to get over the trauma they would experience. Moreover, I would have gone through all those feelings way earlier than them, and they would be facing those feelings only much later and we would be so far away from each other, as far as emotions and feelings were considered. For example, some parents who were to cross the Maritza river had described that road trip as if it was a touristic tour. I explained to my children all the risks. Fear, anxiety, and whatever else was out there, we had to live it together.

We had contacted some friends who had crossed Maritza river earlier to leave Turkey and eventually got in touch with the human smugglers. Then came the preparation stage! First, I ordered three life jackets online. I also bought a very thick rope to tie my children together so that in case of a problem, my son, who was the only one in our household who knew how to swim, could pull his sister ashore. My son and I would carry two backpacks, so I put the important documents and spare clothes in them, together with some items belonging to Gokhan which would remind us of him, like his small prayer rug, his kufi cap, and his Quran...

I often thought of Bayram Yüksel[38] who participated in the Korean War in 1950s. When he was to leave Turkey, he had taken with him his beloved Master Said Nursi's robe. During the war, when he was caught in the middle of a forest fire, he had put the robe on and shouted towards the flames, "Bring it on! Can you burn me in this robe?" God had blessed him and took him out of that hell, safe and secure. Just like that, I took Gokhan's prayer rug with me, which was sent by dear Fethullah Gulen some time ago, as if to say "Bring it on Maritza! Bring it on!"

We were going to leave on Wednesday, April 18, 2018. It was like a funeral coming out of the house. The whole family gathered at my brother's place, and my dear father cried nonstop. My sister and I were packing the backpacks. We put flashlights, mosquito repellent that we knew we would definitely need as we walked through paddy fields on the border, a few bottles of water, and a small amount of food and nuts. Just in case the backpacks

---

38 Bayram Yuksel (1931-1997) is one of the companions of Said Nursi.

Even if the wind blows forever, the mountain never shakes!

fell into the water, we wrapped everything in plastic bags so they would not get wet.

It was my son's midterm exam day. We were leaving that afternoon, but I sent him to school to take his exam in the morning. He didn't want to and said, "Why? We are leaving anyhow!" But I had to consider every possibility. I did not want him to lose a year at school if somehow we could not make it. Even if we were caught and I went to jail, he should have continued with his school.

There is an old saying which goes as: "Farewells are worse than death." Well, we had seen both of them already. Everyone was quiet as stone. Even though we looked at each other's faces, nothing came out of anyone's mouth. I was about to say, "Forgive me for anything that…" but it felt as if a lump blocked my throat. Maybe this was the last time that we were seeing each other. My dad was still crying. My mother turned to me, "Please try to eat something, you're going to collapse on the road!"

We hugged each other, cried, and prayed. Usually the goodbyes take long, but I cut it short and said goodbye to all of them very fast. I knew I'd never be able to leave if I were to hang around for a little bit. I didn't know it that day, and I probably wouldn't have left if I'd known, but this was going to be the last time I would hug my father.

My hero, my greatest supporter, my dear dad would pass away while I was abroad, and I wouldn't even be able to attend his funeral.

MARITZA MORE MERCIFUL THAN THE TURKISH JUSTICE?

We would meet with the human smuggler at 7:00 p.m. With our backpacks on our shoulders, we were waiting for our fate, nervously. Then a Jeep drove up and we got in. After 15 minutes, the driver dropped us at the side of a plantation field, we paid the money and got off. There was another smuggler waiting for us there, together with another family of five. We walked through the fields for two and a half hours. It was getting dark when we arrived to a place where some farmers were working nearby. We hid in the bushes for some time and waited. We didn't want to be seen. Who knows, one of them could call the local police. While waiting, we performed our evening prayers. Mosquitos were attacking nonstop, despite the repellents. We did not talk unless it was necessary…patiently waited, whispering our prayers.

We were going to keep walking after it turned really dark, and the villagers returned to their homes. Even the adults in the group were exhausted, but neither my daughter nor the other two small children in the group complained about anything, not even once. Well, it was not a walk in the park, it was very tough. The smuggler was walking so fast in front of us, we could hardly catch up with him. My dear son Fatih was trying to help me, reaching out every now and then: "Let me carry your bag, Mom." And sometimes, I was trying to help him.

Just when we began walking on a road, we saw in the distance a car approaching towards us with its headlights on. The smuggler gave a mouthful, "Those …!!! They've called the cops! We are done!" We did the only thing that we could: we prayed. The car passed us, thank God. It was not the police.

We kept walking, but we were so scared. Every time we saw a vehicle, we hid or crouched down. And after a while the smuggler left us, saying that he would look for an offroad path. We had already paid him. What would we do by ourselves if he left us right there, in the middle of nowhere?

After waiting next to a wheat field for about 15 minutes, thankfully he came back. After walking a little further, we met with a local young man who was not a Turk. Eventually, they had hidden a boat somewhere close earlier, they took it out and began to carry it. We were just following them. I thought that when we got close to the river, they would let us know us so we could put on our life jackets. But we had already come to the banks of the river and were rushed to the boat. One by one, we got into the boat. I noticed that every time someone got in, the boat was getting more unstable. Moreover, it was pretty wet inside the boat, which was clearly overloaded. I was so scared that the boat might sink.

The boat had already left the shore when I reached for my daughter's life jacket in the backpack and put it on her. Then my son and I put them on. When I threw away the empty backpack, in which we had carried the life jackets, I realized that the thick rope was gone as well. I couldn't tie my daughter and son together as I had planned in case the boat capsized.

When I had talked earlier to a few people who fled through the Maritza river, they had said that the boats were sinking mostly because they got stuck in the roots of trees and punctured. That was always on my mind, when our boat was moving forward in the river contacting with many different things. I have to admit, I was pretty worried when the boat eventually got stuck in a tree root for a while. When the smuggler got off the boat to check it, I noticed that the depth in that part of the river was only up to his neck. I relaxed a little bit and thought, "Well, if

Even if the wind blows forever, the mountain never shakes!

the boat sinks, at least the water's not too deep here."

About ten minutes later, I was relieved when the boat approached the land. We had crossed the river so quickly! I thought we were in Greece now. But I was wrong! After a few minutes of walking, the smugglers took the boat down in the river again. It was pitch black around and I had not noticed it, but apparently the part of the river that we just crossed was only a tributary. We were now to cross the main part of the Maritza river, which was flowing in front of us in all its eeriness…and contrary to what I had thought, it was very deep!

While the smuggler was rowing, he kept warning us: "Don't make a sound, crouch down!" Just then, my daughter dropped her knitted doll into the river and got very upset. Since she was a toddler, she was carrying it wherever we had gone. After another 15 minutes, the smuggler pulled the boat to a secluded place at the bottom of a steep slope. He said, "Get off!" but it was nearly impossible to do so! The slope was so steep and fully covered with thorns and prickles. It was me who was sitting closest to the land so I somehow managed to get off the boat. Grabbing on the bushes full of prickles, I climbed the hill and helped others. The sharp prickles had cut my hands all over. It was so difficult, but when we climbed that hill and saw the land of Greece in front of us, we all breathed a sigh of relief and said, "Alhamdulillah!"[39]

NO BATHROOM FOR 26 HOURS!

It was around 10:30 p.m., there were some weak lights flickering in the distance, but it was utterly dark around us. Before leaving us, the smugglers had warned us: "Try to walk inland as much as you can…if you are caught close to the river, they will send you back!" So, we were trying to be as quiet as possible and get away from the shore. There were eight of us. My son opened the map of Greece on his phone, and we began walking. We didn't use our flashlights unless it was absolutely necessary to do so.

We had walked for two and a half hours earlier, before we crossed the river on the boat. And afterward, we walked through a forest in Greece for another four and a half hours. After a while, we decided to follow the road. Whenever we noticed the headlights of a car approaching, we were throwing ourselves to the shoulder of the road and hiding. Since we were so exhausted, it was taking us at least 10 minutes to get on our feet again, whenever we crouched down in a ditch at the side of the

---

39 Arabic phrase meaning "Praise be to God."

Even if the wind blows forever, the mountain never shakes!

road.

We were nervous and exhausted, and the night was freezing cold. So, we decided to take a rest and meanwhile performed our night prayers. Some changed their muddy clothes. Everyone had brought something to eat in their backpacks; we shared what we had. When we began walking again, I realized I couldn't feel my left leg as it had become numb. It was normal after a seven-hour walk, though.

For hours, whenever we saw a car approaching, we were hiding. But now, being completely exhausted, we didn't mind anymore when cars were passing us every now and then. After a while, a white van stopped next to us and I thought: "What a good person! He will help us! God bless him!" And then I heard someone shouting: "Police!" and got dumbstruck in fear.

The van, with no rear door and no windows, made a U-turn after picking us up, and we went back on the exact same road we had walked. At some point we said to each other: "We walked so many hours for nothing!" After a while, we came to the village which we had walked through a few hours ago when all the dogs in the village had barked at us nonstop, for minutes. There was a café in the village with chairs in front of it. A few hours ago, we had thought of sitting on the chairs for a while to rest, but then we had changed our mind because we had not got permission from the owner of the café.

We were brought to the police station of that village. The first thing we saw when they took us out of the van was a truck which was full of Syrians. The police was not treating them well at all while unloading them from the truck. My son and another man in our group tried to speak English to the police and told them that we fled Turkey for political asylum. The police treated us much better and to comfort us, they even said that Erdogan was nothing but a dictator.

We were taken to a waiting room with old, dusty benches in it, cobwebs hanging from the ceiling. The detention rooms were full of Syrians who were brought in right before us. We were so tired that we couldn't even hold up our heads, but we didn't want to lie down because the room was so filthy.

When we walked in, we saw a family of five sitting in a corner. They were like us, just escaped from Turkey. There were five of them, eight of us, and an Azeri man, somehow wounded, who spent the night in that room. The policeman who attended us there knew almost everything related to Turkey's political agenda. He talked about

Even if the wind blows forever, the mountain never shakes!

Erdogan and Bahceli being complicit in the same sin, and for a moment he even stopped and asked, "Do you have ByLock[40] on your phones?" Then he continued: "Even I am afraid to go to the shore of the Maritza. Erdogan recently violated the border again and kidnapped a few of our soldiers."

They didn't give us food because we arrived late at night. That didn't matter, but before the sunrise in the morning we had to perform our morning prayer, and the sinks and toilets were in the other part of the building where the detention rooms were located. Children had used a dark corner of the yard, but that day adults would not have access to a restroom for 26 hours! We had to perform ablution[41] before the morning prayer, but there was no way of doing it. Then we saw a dusty brick we found in a corner and made tayammum[42] with it. The

---

40 ByLock is a smartphone application that allowed users to communicate via a private connection. It was launched in 2014 on Google Play and Apple App Store, it was permanently shut down in March 2016. Turkish authorities claim that ByLock is exclusively used by members of the Hizmet movement to ensure the privacy of their conversations. Users of ByLock were considered as terrorists in Turkish courts.
41 The Islamic procedure for cleansing parts of the body, a type of ritual purification. The mandatory acts of ablution consists of washing the face, arms, and feet with water and wiping the head.
42 The Islamic act of dry ritual purification using sand (or earth), which may be performed in place of ritual ablution if no clean water is readily available, by placing the palms of your hands on the sand and rubbing your face and back of your hands with the palms of your hands.

floor was really dirty and not suitable to pray on it, but there was an old door that was thrown aside on another corner. So, we performed our prayer on it.

When I consider it in retrospect, I say "How difficult everything was!" But that day, I had not complained about anything, and neither anyone else did. Because we had left Turkey and we were finally free! We had managed to cross the Maritza! We had survived! Thank God!

After some time, they took us into the main detention hall when they took some of the Syrians to the refugee camp. There were around 50 people in the hall, maybe two-thirds of them were Syrians. It was really crowded, we had to pull our knees to our chest while sitting to barely fit. And let me tell you, that place was incredibly filthy! The blankets were stinking, and there were dead insects all over the place. I found a corner and waited there, together with my children.

In the following hours during the day, it became so hot inside that it was simply unbearable. And those Syrians were talking so loud to each other that my daughter eventually began crying and said: "Why are we staying here? Let's go somewhere else!" Hours have passed like that until late evening when we performed the night prayer in congregation. That is when we had some

Even if the wind blows forever, the mountain never shakes!

kind of peace and relief, albeit for a short period of time.

Of course, I could not lie down comfortably with all the people around, but I was feeling so exhausted that I just curled up in the corner and tried to catch some sleep. That is when I had a migraine attack, and whatever I did, it didn't ease down. As we tried to sleep, the Syrians were chatting loudly, laughing and joking among themselves. I was about to go crazy. A few people in our group asked them kindly to be quiet, but it didn't help. At one point, I looked at them and asked them in Arabic to be please quiet, but one of them snapped at me in a broken Turkish, saying, "Just go to sleep, will you?" It was so weird, some of them were sleeping while the others were chatting, laughing loudly and shouting at each other. After a while they would get tired and go to sleep and the first group would wake up and continue with the loud conversation. It was just insane! Both their noise and my migraine lasted until morning.

WE WILL NOT QUIT SERVING FOR OUR NATION

We spent three nights there, in that detention hall. After the first night, they had taken the Syrians to the refugee camps. It was only thirteen of us left. But then, it became significantly cold inside the hall, to the extent that we began to snuggle up in our coats and reaching for the dirty blankets that we hadn't even touched for two days. We did our best to keep the kids warm so they wouldn't catch a cold and get sick.

The breakfast menu was pretty fixed: a piece of bread with cheddar cheese in it, juice, and croissants. For dinner, they served pickled beets, green beans, and chicken rice, which we didn't touch of course because it was not *halal*[43] meat.

Who knows how many people had stayed in that detention center on their journey to hope? Just looking at the scripts on the walls of the hall was enough to give you an idea. There were so many names and signatures on the walls, so many things written in so many different languages. Those dirty walls would bear witness to the history of refugees in some way. Our eyes looked for a few familiar words, and then we saw it, written in Turkish: "*Abiler, ablalar biz de buradaydık.*"[44] It was smiling at us like a close friend. Well, since there was such a tradition, we wanted to keep it going. There was an old bench in

---
43 Arabic word for "permissible". *Halal* meat refers refer to the slaughter and preparation of meat in accordance with Islamic practices.
44 Turkish for "Brothers and sisters, we were here, too!"

Even if the wind blows forever, the mountain never shakes!

the corner, and one of our group members stepped on it and scratched on the wall with the coin in his hand the following:

"*Çıktık dikenli yollara*

Söz verdik Allah'a

Ermeden mevsim bahara

Geri dönmeyiz"[45]

My son and I wanted to write something, too. We thought for a while about what to write. Then I remembered a verse from Namık Kemal's[46] *Ode of Freedom*. Although I knew these verses before, it really made much more sense to me when I had heard it from Esma Demirhan some time ago, whose husband was unlawfully arrested and then sentenced to life in prison during the 17/25 December Corruption Operations[47]. That's what

---
45 "On the roads covered with thorns…
We promised God the Almighty;
We shall not turn back…
Until we reach the Spring!"

46 Namık Kemal (1840 – 1888) was an Ottoman writer, intellectual, reformer, journalist, playwright, and political activist who was influential in the formation of the Young Ottomans and their struggle for governmental reform in the Ottoman Empire during the late 19th century. Kemal was particularly significant for championing the notions of freedom and fatherland in his numerous plays and poems, and his works would have a powerful impact on the establishment of and future reform movements in Turkey.

47 The December 17-25, 2013, corruption scandal in Turkey refers to a criminal investigation that involves several key people in the Turkish

my son and I scratched on those black walls.

"*Felek esbab-ı cefasın toplasın gelsin.*

Dönersek namerdiz millet yolunda bir azimetten"[48]

Two other Turkish families joined us on our last day in that detention hall. As two-day-old "locals", this time we hosted them. The seeds of the friendship planted that day would bear fruit afterward. Much later on, we would meet with one of those families again and be close friends.

My daughter was so overwhelmed on the first day in the detention hall, but then thankfully she got kind of used to it. One of the friends in our group had brought some Indian henna in her backpack. God bless her, she kept the children busy with henna and told them stories. There's indeed such a thing called "the innocence of a child." The kids got used to the environment quickly, laughing and playing together. As for the adults, our psychology was quite different: we were crying at one moment and then the next moment, we were all smiling. Also, it was

---

government. Prosecutors accused 14 people, including several family members of the cabinet ministers, the director of state-owned bank (Halkbank) and Turkish-Iranian businessman Reza Zarrab, of bribery, corruption, fraud, money laundering and gold smuggling. In March 2016, Reza Zarrab was arrested in Miami. In November 2017, Zarrab cooperated with federal prosecutors and has become key witness in the case of money laundering and violating sanctions on Iran.

48 "May the fate gather all kinds of hardships,
   We will never give up serving for our nation."

Even if the wind blows forever, the mountain never shakes!

such a weird situation because everyone was kind of afraid of each other. No one revealed their full identity to the others, nor did they give detailed information about themselves. After everything we had been through, we all shared and understood each other's concerns.

The police officers often visited us asking, "Do you need anything?" They gave a few small balls to the kids through the iron bars of the main door. Later, they brought some chocolate alongside a few water bottles. Although we had to throw the chocolate away because of the alcohol in its ingredients, we appreciated their sincere kindness. It touched our hearts to see better treatment here in Greece, when we were not even considered as human beings in Turkey, our own country!

FATIGUE OF HARD TIMES ON MY SHOULDERS...

It was Saturday. You know how the Greeks are kind of relaxed and cool people in general. Their morning shift starts not until 10:00 am, and they still have a siesta at 3:00 pm. So we thought, "There is no way that they will release us until Monday." Food, water, performing the daily prayers, the use of bathrooms…pretty much everything was a problem in the detention center, but we were patiently waiting for days. Well, to our huge surprise, a police officer came late in the morning of that Saturday and said "All done, we will let you out soon."

They returned our belongings to us in full and asked where we were going. We said, "Thessaloniki." They called a few taxis which would take us to the bus station and warned us: "Don't forget to negotiate with the drivers about the taxi fare!"

It was around noon when we arrived to the bus station and bought our tickets. Tired and heavy-hearted, I looked deep into my soul, while traveling in the bus with my children, with my head leaned against the bus window. I was free now! I was feeling relieved, although not quite fully. We were together as a family, except of course our dear Gokhan missing. Then I noticed one thing: Even when I was traveling on the bus, I was getting startled and my legs were trembling whenever I saw a police car passing us. If you ask, "When did this end?" the answer is, it didn't! I still feel like that! I've been here for more than three years, but I still feel anxious every time I see the police.

During the five-hour bus ride, I had chatted with my children or got lost in thoughts. The towns that we were passing by were looking so similar to the towns in Turkey.

Even if the wind blows forever, the mountain never shakes!

Sometimes we were entering into a small village to drop off a passenger. The houses were so similar, we saw even minarets of small mosques every now and then and got excited. We passed through the city of Alexandrium (Dimetoka in the Ottoman period) and talked to each other commenting about the mountains around, the landscape, and the plantation fields. At that time, we were so heartbroken that we felt like we were never going to miss our country. I guess we needed some time to miss what we left behind.

When we arrived at the Thessaloniki bus station, an old friend was waiting for us. I had contacted her earlier and told her when we were coming. She took us to her home. We were covered in dirt and incredibly tired. We took showers, had dinner, drank tea and chatted. Our dirty clothes were already in the laundry, we had washed our muddy shoes and left them to dry. We called my parents and let them know that we were doing fine. A hope was growing inside us and we were wishing that things would go back to normal somehow. It felt really nice that I was sitting there with my dear friend, and we were having a conversation without any fear in us. Just like in the good old days. What do two friends talk about when they get back together after a long time? We talked about our good memories of the past, about my dear Gokhan, whom I still can't believe was murdered, and the Maritza river. We cried and laughed…and then cried some more.

That was how our two-month adventure in Thessaloniki began. My friend's husband took us for a walk on the beach in the morning. Oh, how much I had missed walking on a beach without having any fear. We bought corn and cotton candy for the kids from the street vendors, and we wandered through the city all day long.

After staying at my friend's place for a few days, we found a house on Airbnb and moved there. It was a lovely little house. Through the kitchen balcony, you could go down to the backyard where there were flowers, stunted trees, and a bench. Sometimes I sat on that bench together with my children and friends and had some tea. There was a shopping mall about a mile away, we were going there for our needs. We were getting daily milk, half of which I was using to make yogurt and the other half we were drinking. It was interesting that for the first time in a long time, we felt that we were indeed getting some pleasure when we were eating and drinking. There was a beach near the house, and my children and I went walking there every day, taking deep breaths all the way in.

The house that we rented had two bedrooms, a living room, and a kitchen. It was furnished, there were familiar items around, of the kind found in a typical Anatolian house: a wooden console table, a glass and wood TV stand, two armchairs, a sofa, and a mini-TV. There were a few photos on the wall. With a Turkish style *fez* on his head, *shalwar* style trousers, and rubber shoes, an old man was looking at us in the photo frame who probably had passed away a long time ago. He was no different than any other old man living in Anatolia. When I asked our hosts, two sisters, about the man in the photo, they told me that he was their great-grandfather who was expelled from Turkey during one of the mass deportations much earlier. There was another photo on the wall, taken during a street wedding. I could swear that photo was taken in a Turkish town, it was so similar, it smelled home.

There was a farmer's market set up near our house once a week, and I was going there with my children. But you needed to be there before 2 pm, otherwise you would come back empty-handed. It was impossible to find anything after that time because it was siesta time between 3-5 pm.

Days were passing by, but we had to draw a road map soon for ourselves, decide what to do, where to go and settle down. But I chose not to rush; after all, the only thing we had experienced in the last two years was a deep grief. I wanted to take a breather first and have some rest together with my children.

We lived for a while doing nothing and thinking about nothing. In the mornings, we were going for a walk on the beach, then shopping, and reading books together. I was happy to see again the big smiles lighting up my children's faces. Yes, we could not make clear plans for the future, we could not even have some dreams about the future because everything was so uncertain in our lives…but, we had hope! I was no more getting worried about those questions like "When will the police come to our house? What about the court trials? Will I be imprisoned?" I was enjoying the time that I was spending with my children. We were brewing tea, eating sunflower seeds on the balcony, and watching the spring rain. Our apartment was on the first floor of the building, so when we were sitting on the balcony, we were greeting the other residents while they were entering or exiting the building. An old man who took his dog out for a walk every evening would tell us *"Kalinixta"* (Greek phrase meaning "Have a good night") on his return. We were wondering where he was if we had not seen him in the evening.

It was April 23rd when we had moved into our first Airbnb apartment in Greece. By mid-May, we had moved to another Airbnb place. And when the holy month of

Even if the wind blows forever, the mountain never shakes!

Ramadan[49] started, we were in another place. That's when we hosted a friend of mine with three kids in our small apartment for four days, since her agreement with Airbnb had just expired. Those first days of the Ramadan were so lovely and peaceful, we enjoyed them so much. Just like in Turkey, I even began to invite guests for dinner, including the people I had just met. In order to be able to feel Ramadan fully, I was reading the entire Quran once a week, just like Osman bin Affan[50] used to do. I can't forget that first Ramadan abroad, reading Quran, preparing food, *taraweeh*[51] and *tahajjud*[52] prayers. It was indeed the month of blessings!

After the dinners, I was taking a walk with my son and daughter on the beach, and sometimes I was catching myself getting worried and thinking: "What if the *MIT*[53]

---

49 Ramadan is the ninth month of the Islamic calendar, observed by Muslims worldwide as a month of fasting, prayer, reflection and community.

50 Osman bin Affan (579 – 656) was one of the companions of Prophet Muhammad (Peace be upon Him). He was the fourth person to embrace Islam and played a major role in early Islamic history as he ruled as the third Caliph between 644-656. He is known for having ordered the compilation of the first standard version of the Quran.

51 Taraweeh prayers are performed only during the month of Ramadan, typically in congregation and around 2 hours after the sunset, depending on the lunar calendar.

52 Tahajjud, also known as the "night prayer", is a voluntary prayer performed by followers of Islam. It is not one of the five obligatory prayers required of all Muslims, although the the Prophet Muhammad (Pecae be upon Him) was recorded as performing the tahajjud prayer regularly himself and encouraging his companions too.

53 Abbreviation of *Milli Istihbarat Teskilati*, Turkish State Intelligence Agency.

is around?" But still, after everything that I had been through, after all those hardships, Thessaloniki became like the cave of the *Ashab al Kahf*[54] for me. I found peace there, I had the best Ramadan of my life there. Thessaloniki was where my wounds healed. But it was time now to take a new path in life and find a permanent home place for myself and my family.

---

54 Arabic phrase for "Companions of the Cave", othjerwise known as Seven Sleepers is about a group of youths who hid inside a cave outside a city to escape one of the Roman persecutions of Christians and emerged some 300 years later.

Chapter 7

A Fresh Start
or
An Inevitable Ending?

The Life and Legacy of Gokhan Acikkollu

FROM ONE CAMP TO ANOTHER...

After living in Greece for two months, we moved to another European country which would eventually be our new homeland. At first, we didn't know what we would do in this new place, but we wanted to stay here for a while and evaluate our options meanwhile.

To tell the truth, where I was leaving didn't really matter to me. My only criterion was that it should be a place where I could feel freedom living together with my children. So, I left it to my children to decide where to live. Since my daughter Zeynep was still young, I asked my son Fatih to decide on a college. We were going to settle down wherever he wanted to go to college. We stayed for a week at a friend's apartment and walked around the city. Then we made our decision and chose this city as our new homeland! There was a great university which Fatih wanted to attend, but also we were really impressed by the people living around who were greeting us with genuine smiles on their faces.

June 25th, 2018... Not long ago, only two years earlier, if we were told that we would officially apply for asylum in a European country, we would probably have laughed, wondering: "Why? How?" But that was what happened soon and we were placed in a refugee camp. Immediately afterward, we hired a Turkish lawyer who was an expert in the field of immigration.

When you are a refugee in a European country, it's not like that there are no hardships anymore. First of all, while your case is being processed, they don't allow you to stay in the same camp more than a few days, in order not to make the refugee status attractive to people. We had stayed in a camp for two days where we had officially applied for the refugee status. After two days, in order to scan our fingerprints and to make an interview, we were taken to another camp. And after two days there, we were transferred yet to another camp.

Our third camp was consisting of bungalow-style duplex houses. It was surprising to see there a family from Konya, whom we had met so many years ago. In that third camp, we stayed for two months. This was a big camp which seemed more like a resort with farms and gardens around it. There was a school inside it, a gym, trails, and bicycle paths.

They gave us a debit card into which a certain amount of money was deposited each week, based on the number of people in the family. Some Syrian men had started a company, they were bringing grocery items to the camp with trucks. We were purchasing our needs from these trucks which were coming on Mondays, Wednesdays, and Fridays. There was also a grocery store near the camp selling organic products, but we didn't go there except for urgent needs because it was a bit expensive.

In this camp we had nothing to do but wait. One day when I was chatting with a friend in the camp, I said to her, "There are so many needy friends left in Turkey. What can we do for them besides praying?" When I was dismissed from my job in Turkey, I had earned a living by making and selling noodles. Why weren't we doing the same thing here? Soon afterward we purchased flour and eggs, we were making noodles and filling them in plastic bags. We spread the word all over the camp, and soon we had to work overtime to catch up with the orders. In the two months we stayed there, we were able to make 1300 euros and send it to our needy friends back in Turkey. All Praise be to God!

Two months later we were transferred to another camp, and hence we got separated from our old friends from Konya. Our new camp was more like an official building with a long hallway inside, rooms on one side, and kitchens on the other. There were two rooms in a so-called "unit", one room for four people and one for two people. We were staying in a room for four. There were two Iranian men in the room for two. There was a shared toilet and bathroom inside the unit, and five units were sharing a kitchen. After we cooked in the kitchen, we were bringing the food to our room and eating there.

We stayed in that camp for three months, from August 30 to November 30. Its location was amazing, inside a peaceful forest. It happens to be that this was a touristic resort earlier, and we were staying there and without paying anything! How about that? We couldn't be thankful enough. I would go for walks with my friends; hike the woods with my children to pick chestnuts, and cook them in the camp.

We certainly cannot repay our sisters and brothers who had moved to this country so many years ago. They supported us so much during our stay in the camp and never left us alone. They made it their duty to take care of us despite their busy daily schedule. We never felt lonely. God bless them forever!

At the end of November we moved to our fifth camp. In this new camp, the kitchen was again to be shared but this time we had our own bathroom adjacent to our room which was a great luxury for us. Actually, performing ablution[55] in the shared bathrooms was

---

55 The Islamic procedure for cleansing parts of the body, a type of ritual purification. The mandatory acts of ablution consists of washing the face, arms, and feet with water and wiping the head.

extremely difficult for women in *hijabs*. There were two things we were looking for in a camp: Can we cook our own food? And how is the bathroom setting? This camp was quite comfortable in that respect, thank God.

Refugees from so many different nationalities were staying in these camps, and they were all very generous in helping each other. When I was making bread, I was leaving some part of it in the kitchen so that some others could enjoy it, too. There was a Shia-Azeri-Iranian teenager who was getting pretty emotional when he was eating that freshly baked bread and saying: "Just like my dear mother's bread." I was trying to give him more bread and he was thanking in his own way by taking out the trash bags during my kitchen cleaning shift. Especially when Fatih was not around, he was definitely there to help.

There were a lot of Turkish families in our last camp. The kids were incredibly happy to find playmates. That was good for me, too. We were together with friends of the same worldview and even started a weekly Quran study group which was really helping us to keep our priorities straight and to have our hearts connected to God. We were hiking around together, organizing birthday parties for our children, and attending the language class in the camp two days a week. A local volunteer was providing language classes in a Hizmet movement-affiliated institution and we were attending those classes, too. So, we were pretty busy with many different activities and this helped us to learn the local language in a short amount of time.

It had been eight months since we started wandering from this camp to that camp. And then, we finally received our interview date: February 12th. The interview was not a formality, at all. As a matter of fact, it was taking four days. We were taking a bus at 6 am in the morning to arrive at the government building in downtown, where the interviews took place. After a very busy schedule, we were brought back to the camp in the evening.

INTERVIEW PROCESS BEGINS

Our interview process was to begin on February 12th, but before that, there was an intensive preparation period. We were completing our missing documents, having preliminary meetings with our lawyer and going over the details of what we had been through in the last several years.

During our stays at each camp, there was a different main agenda. For example, in the previous camp the conversation topic was pretty much around the question

"Have you received your interview date yet?" In this camp, we were trying to talk to those who had already gone through the interview process to benefit from their experience. The questions were now like "What did they ask about in the interview? How should we answer them? What should we do about this, about that?"

We would leave the camp very early in the morning and come back late in the evening. It would have been exhausting for my daughter, both physically and emotionally. I wrote and sent a petition to the Migration Administration stating, "I consider it more appropriate for my daughter to stay together with my friend in the camp during the interview process." Thankfully it was accepted. So it was me and my son Fatih only who went to the daily interviews.

On the first day of the interview, they asked questions like "How did you get to Greece? How did you get here?" Meanwhile, they were examining all the documents I had previously sent to them - our marriage certificate, Gokhan's death certificate, school diplomas, court documents, etc.

On the second day, when we arrived in the morning, we first met with our lawyer and worked on the files. One last time we went over everything together, made the necessary revisions, and took care of some minor problems mostly related to the translation mistakes.

The third and most important day was when the main interview would be held. They asked questions like, "Why did you come here? Why did you leave your country? What kind of affiliations do you have?" Their main goal was to understand whether we were really of those people that the Erdogan government has persecuted. In their words, the question was: "Are you indeed connected with the Hizmet movement?" Being connected to Hizmet was enough evidence for the Erdogan government to label you as a terrorist in Turkey. In a country where the rule of law was upheld, on the other hand, the same very connection was enough evidence that you were innocent and thus you were provided permanent residency. How tragic for Turkey!

Reciting the Qur'an, praying, attending Quran study groups, helping needy people and students, not stealing, not lying…all of these were considered as evidence of your connection with the Hizmet movement in New Turkey's justice system and you were treated as criminals. But here, in this country of law, where we took refuge fleeing from the oppression in Turkey, the above-mentioned acts were the necessary conditions in order for your asylum application to be accepted.

The Life and Legacy of Gokhan Acikkollu

PAINTING WINDOW FRAMES AT THE SUMMIT OF MY CAREER!

The four-day interview process I mentioned above was so painful, but not only because that it started early in the morning and lasted until late in the evening. The real reason was that they wanted us to tell every detail of what we had been through in the last years, and we felt like that we were living all those traumas again.

My friends had told me that they were asked questions like, "Write down the names of Fethullah Gülen's books! Which of these have you read? What were their contents? Which one were you most impressed with? How many children does Fethullah Gülen have? What's his wife's name?" They didn't ask us any questions like these. My son's interview was short, but mine took a long time. We went over everything that happened over and over again, and it truly exhausted me psychologically.

After the fourth and final day, they told us there would be a waiting period. As soon as our interviews were over, they transferred us from that "IND camp" to another place. And shortly afterward, we were taken to our sixth and final camp. Now all that was left was to wait for the permanent residency status.

Exactly one month after the end of the interviews, on

A Fresh Start or An Inevitable Ending?

March 16th, I received a message from my lawyer: "We've received the permanent residency!" I felt a bittersweet joy. After our application last year on June 25, 2018, we had stayed in the camps for a period of nine months.

It was just a matter of some procedure that was left, such as applying to the camp officials with our documents, choosing the district we wanted to live in, and telling the officials why we preferred that district. We chose our district based on the criteria that it was close to my son's university and a few friends' houses.

There was not a standard time period for this last process, it could be different from case to case but thankfully it didn't take long for us. At the beginning of April, on a Wednesday, our choice of district was approved. Only a week later, we were assigned our house. This was such an important and pleasant step in getting back to a normal life. Everything here was following a clear procedure, step by step. The home office made an appointment with us, we just went and picked up the keys of our house.

In Turkey, everything was different with respect to finding a house, buying, or renting it. Here the procedure was quite different and also kind of troublesome. The houses around were so old and people sometimes had to wait for years to find a house. I addition, it was not unusual that when you moved in to your new house, you would see that the previous resident had taken many things with him when he left the house: Kitchen appliances, floor tiles, light bulbs, wallpaper and many other things. We were supposed to refurbish them all.

The city gave us a loan to renovate the house which looked pretty ruined when we saw it for the first time. It took us one and a half months to renovate it. We purchased new kitchen appliances from a website which was selling used house items, replaced the floor tiles and all the light bulbs, and applied three or four layers of plasters on the walls. And we did all this with the help of our brothers and sisters living around. They never left us alone. May God bless them!

We continued to stay in the camp during the renovation of the house. My son and I were leaving the camp early in the morning, working all day long to clean the house and to repair things around. I painted the frames of the windows myself. On one of those days, I took a picture of the window frames that I was painting and shared it in my WhatsApp status with a message: "I studied for 17 years, worked for 23 years. Now I'm painting window frames at the peak of my career."

A Fresh Start or An Inevitable Ending?

Every evening we would come to the camp, exhausted and covered in dust. Normally, after you are assigned a house, you're given two weeks to leave the camp. However, since the renovation of the house did not finish, I asked from the camp administration to stay in the camp for two more weeks. Well, they gave us only one more week. That was not enough for us to finish our job in the house, but we left the camp after that extra week. We stayed in the house of a friend for a week and then stayed another week with another friend. It was the end of May when we finally moved into our own home.

A DIFFERENT MEMORY IN EACH BOX

After living in at least ten different places in one year, we finally were living in our own home, and we were so thankful and grateful. An air mattress and two floor cushions were our first pieces of furniture and they were given to us by a friend. I can't forget that first dinner we had in our place. I was cooking something simple on the electric stove, when the doorbell rang. My dear sisters had come with their hands full of food plates!

On the second evening in our house, this time I invited them to dinner. They became our first guests at home. We laid a cloth on the floor and enjoyed our dinner together: green lentil soup with noodles, meat sauté, and rice.

We had to wait until the third day for our house to look like a real home because that is when our furniture and belongings arrived from Turkey. We were in a city of a foreign country, in a house that we had almost rebuilt working like a construction worker for one and a half months…and seeing our old belongings and furniture under these conditions was just priceless! It felt like seeing a dear old friend, like smelling your old home that you had lived in, in the good old days. There was the sofa set with hundreds of memories on it…and here is the corner of the sofa where Gokhan used to lie down…the coffee table that witnessed so many lovely conversations…our bookshelf, our books that we read and shared with each other. All these furniture items were smelling actually of ourselves, of our laughters, our joy, our happy days, our hope…and yes, also our grief, our longing, and our hope.

I had been waiting eagerly for the furniture to arrive, but when I was opening the boxes, I felt a moment of regret and thought, "I wish I hadn't brought them here." Especially when I opened the box in which Gokhan's clothes were packed, I couldn't stop the tears coming out of my eyes. It was such a weird and painful feeling to see the clothes of your loved one who was no longer with you. Crying just like that, in sadness and grief, I didn't see my daughter walking into the room. When I noticed her I turned my back to hide my tears, but she came over, hugging me tightly from behind. "I know why you're crying, Mom" she said, "You're crying because you saw my father's clothes." For the first time, I was caught offhand and could not even tell her anything. It was me until that day who had always comforted her, but that day, for the first time, my dear Zeynep comforted me. She calmed me down and reminded me of my words, "Would you want to be with him for a short time period in this world, or would you want to be with him in the Hereafter, forever? We will meet with him in the Hereafter, don't be sad Mommy, please."

For the first couple of days, I was sad and regretted it, but then I changed my mind gradually and said, "I'm glad I brought all our belongings." We were so familiar with all of those items, our sofas, our bookshelf, everything. It became much easier for us to get used to our new home with all the familiar items in it now.

WIPING THE SLATE CLEAN?

You know how it's called "a *new* country and a *fresh* beginning." I think the word "beginning" fits only for children. Well, my children both began to speak this new language in a short amount of time. My son Fatih wants to be a computer engineer and spends his days learning anything related to computers. Well, he was never a social kid and he didn't usually hang out with his age group. He's pretty mature, knows what he wants, and selective about building friendships.

My daughter attends her new school and I am glad to see that she's been able to make new friends. With the help of the psychological support she receives, she is slowly recovering from the trauma. She's usually fine, but sometimes she has serious breakdowns. The other day, I found her crying and when I asked about the reason, she said: "I have this very strange feeling inside me, I don't know if it is a void in my heart or a longing!" Frequently and patiently, I explain to her that, "Martyrs are not really dead, they're alive. Your father died a martyr. We'll meet in heaven, God willing." On another occasion, she came home crying and said that her friends talked about the gifts their father gave to them. I said, "But darling, your brother and I are buying you many gifts," but she continued to cry and said "You don't understand, I'm telling you, it is their fathers who are buying those gifts! Their fathers!" In these situations, there's nothing left to say. I feel so helpless, especially when my daughter says,

A Fresh Start or An Inevitable Ending?

"I miss saying 'Dad'!" How can you substitute the needs of a child longing for her father, anyhow?

After a certain age, especially when your brain is so tired and preoccupied, it's really hard to learn a new language. That's why I am way behind Fatih and Zeynep. Thankfully, my children were able to make that "new beginning" but I can't see that power in myself. I do most of the things just because I have to.

Everything we lived through belongs now to the past. Or is that so? I guess my answer is both "Yes" and "No." Sometimes I feel fine and strong. Yet sometimes I feel myself sinking deeper and deeper. There are times when I get tired of being strong. Maybe I should let things go a little, I should share my feelings and my troubles with close friends. But I am not good in doing that, either. Though, I often host guests at our home, sometimes even strangers show up just to meet us and have a chat. That helps me a lot.

The phrase "wiping the slate clean" has never made sense for me. I feel like it's impossible to forget about the past, to forget about all the wrongdoings. If a human being exists as a whole with his past, present, and future…then perhaps the right thing to do is not to make a new beginning by covering the past. Maybe one needs to accept things as they are…maybe one needs to say to herself "It is what it is, and there is nothing I can do to change the past." Maybe only then…and with that submission in mind, you can make a new beginning. Who knows?

I sometimes think, "What would I do if they said that we could go back to Turkey without getting worried about anything?" If all the injustices were rectified, if we were reinstated to our jobs, would I accept going back to Turkey? Part of me says "Why not? You can go back to your country and continue where you left off." But there is another part of me saying, "My children's father was brutally murdered in that country. What can that country offer to my children after what happened?" Alas! A part of me and my children will be always empty!

But then again, no matter what we go through, life has to go on somehow. There are a few things that I want to do, I don't know whether I can use the word "dream", or would it be too ambitious to dream of them? Well, my priority is to be fluent in this local language as soon as possible. There are so many volunteer jobs I can do in this country. I could work somewhere as a teacher or a nurse, but sometimes I feel like I don't have the strength for either of them. Sometimes I think, "If I worked in a place involving flowers and gardens, I'd be feeling better." But

A Fresh Start or An Inevitable Ending?

I don't know how satisfying that would be. In short, the future is looking quite foggy. But if there's one thing I'm sure of, it's that I don't have the strength to get involved into anything of a high-stress and challenging nature. I don't have big plans or expectations about the future. I'd just like to do good things in this world and increase the quality of my relationship with God.

Sometimes, they ask, "Do you need psychological support?" I think about it from time to time, especially when I feel like I'm so lost. There are times when I get intolerant and I catch myself scolding the kids when they misbehave. Then I regret and get angry at myself for doing so. Would it be better if I consulted a psychologist or even a psychiatrist? But I'm worried they would prescribe medication for me. I don't want to be on medication every day, walking around with no emotion. And as for the therapy, believe me, I don't have the energy to explain anything to anyone anymore.

Will I make a real fresh start and think about marriage someday? I don't think so. After Gokhan's death, I closed that book, forever. Besides, I don't think there's anyone out there who would carry all this burden with me.

...

No one in my family could visit us yet. They've had different trials in the last two years. First, we lost my brother's wife to a serious disease. From the bottom of my heart, I am a witness for her goodness, for her good heart. God bless her for all the support she had given to me.

My father really wanted to visit us, and he even got passports for him and my mother. However, one day while he was having tea with friends, he suddenly collapsed and died shortly after from a brain hemorrhage. It's easy now for me to write about it, but it was such a shock for me when I had heard about it. I was so shaken, yet one more time, and I am still not fully recovered. I had lost my husband three years before I lost my father, and only after I lost my father, I realized that all this time I couldn't understand my children's feelings. Only then I asked them: "How did you just hang in there? For three years? Oh, how tough it is to live without a father!"

LIFE GOES ON, SO DOES THE LONGING

As much as life seems to be returning to normal, there's a big void in our lives. My children miss their father, and I miss my husband very much. Gokhan is someone irreplaceable, and we have no intention whatsoever of replacing him.

I sometimes feel his absence while sipping tea alone (Gokhan loved tea so much), and sometimes when I see couples walking around holding hands. When I face the difficulties and challenges related to our children, I feel so lonely, weak, and desperate. When I see couples arguing about something, my heart gets in my mouth, and I hardly stop myself from approaching them and telling "Please don't do this! While you're both alive, do appreciate each other! Please!"

If you would ask me, "What do you miss the most about him?" I would say: Drinking tea or coffee together, watching movies until late in the night, going shopping together or on a picnic, our road trips, long breakfasts as a family, getting angry when he spent a lot of time on the computer, making fun of him…pretty much everything about him. All these things look simple and ordinary, and you take them for granted when you live them together with your loved one…but when your loved one dies, that is when you realize how each of them was truly a blessing.

We're human beings, after all. I don't know how much longer I will live in this world, but even in my dreams about the future, Gokhan's place is always missing…our children will celebrate their school graduations without their father. When they make plans to get married, they cannot introduce their fathers to their prospective spouses. Their father will not be there at the wedding, and their children won't know their grandfather. When I think about all these, I face the sad reality: My children will always fly with a broken wing in this world…a broken wing that cannot be fixed. I don't know whether I will live long enough to see those days, but even now I get upset when I think about it. A void which is impossible to fill. You can get used to it, but it doesn't alleviate the pain.

The tests of God don't end until you're under the ground. The phrase "let go of the dead and live your life" is quite frustrating, but there's some truth to it. Yes, you can't eat for days, but you have to eat at some point. You cry nonstop, but at some point you run out of tears. You get up for your children because you are still a mother. You are still a servant of God. As a human, mother, and servant, you still have responsibilities. Being a servant of God, you must keep worshipping Him. Being a mother, you have to take care of your children.

I ask my Lord to give me and all our brothers and sisters strength! May Allah let us pass these worldly tests with success, earning His pleasure! Amen.

Yes, I've been extremely saddened by the fact that our lives have been turned upside down in the last few years, but I'm trying to perceive things from the perspective of destiny and divine test.

But then again, I will never stop seeking for justice and trying to hold those perpetrators accountable for their crimes, both in this world and the next. I will never say "Well, it is just fate, and there is nothing we can do about it." No, I will not step aside!

I will demand justice until justice is done!

Yes, I believe firmly in destiny and the Hereafter, but I also believe that if I let those perpetrators get away with their horrendous crimes, shame on me! Yes, shame on me!

Until my last breath, I will chase the murderers and their bosses!

I will do everything in my power, and if I cannot get any results in this world…

There is a God! There is a Hereafter! There is Divine Justice!

I fully believe!

The Life and Legacy of Gokhan Acikkollu

GOKHAN IS STILL WITH US...

In chapter *Baqara*h of Quran, there is a verse, which reads as: *"Do not say that those who are killed in God's cause are dead; they are alive, though you do not realize it."* I believe that Gokhan is not dead but is still with us. I've dreamed of him many times since he passed away. Every time I ask in my dream, "Aren't you dead?" And he replies: "I did not die, I am just assigned to this place." He once said, "I've been assigned to *Bitlis*[56]." Another time he said, "I'm going to Germany." In another dream, he said to me, "I'll be assigned next to you soon, I've applied for family union." Some other people have seen him in their dreams, too, and they all say the same thing: Gokhan keeps telling: "I am not dead; I am still on duty."

I know Gokhan is still with us, and I always feel he takes care of us. Because whenever I felt so overwhelmed and depressed, I saw him in my dreams, and he comforted me. In none of those dreams, he knew that he was dead. He was saying things like that he is still working, he is assigned to another school in another town, he has applied for family union process to be appointed in a school in our town, etc. Of course, I'm aware that such a union would not be possible in this world under normal conditions.

---

56 A city in southeastern Turkey.

Hence, I hope that I will be assigned next to him for our reunion, when that time comes. My children are equally trying to be worthy of their father. My Gokhan is still alive, among us, benefitting people. May my Lord make us worthy of him!

Shortly after his death, my sister had seen Gokhan in her dream. He was wearing a pure white outfit and holding a notebook tightly in his hand. When my sister asked him "What's that notebook about?" he answered, "This is my intercession list."

My younger brother's recently deceased wife also had a dream about Gokhan and told me about it. In her dream, we had all gone to visit Gokhan's grave, and the soil on the grave was moving up and down like breathing. We opened the grave while screaming "He is not dead, he is alive! He is alive!" and saw Gokhan just like we remember him, lying as if he was on a couch, with his shirt on.

After Gokhan's death, for a long time I didn't sleep during the nights. During a typical day, I wasn't sleeping more than a few hours. I was trying to look strong during the day and not shed a single tear so that both my children and my parents wouldn't be upset. But when it was nighttime and everyone was asleep, that was when I was living my grief to the fullest. I was performing the regular night prayer first, then the *salat'ul haja*[57], later reciting the names of the *Ashab al Badr*[58], saying my supplications, and meanwhile I was crying and crying until my prayer rug was getting wet with my tears. Those were special moments that belonged only to my Lord and me.

It was one of those days when I cried and prayed all night long until morning, I had performed my morning prayer, sitting on the bed. My eyes were burning from crying. Suddenly I heard a noise coming from the bathroom. Someone was performing ablution. I thought, "my mother is getting ready for the prayer." But then I heard the person was mumbling a song. I remember shuddering to my bones because it was Gokhan's voice! I wanted to get up and look, but I was so scared. No, it wasn't a hallucination and no, I was not sleeping at that time. Then I saw him, it was Gokhan! He just walked past the open door of the bedroom and went straight to the

---

57 Arabic phrase for "Prayer of Need". It is a voluntary prayer and usually performed by a Muslim who is in need of something. It is a prayer that raises your need to God and exhibits your neediness and absolute slavehood to Him. When you consign your matters to God, you have faith that He is the Only One who gives you what you need. Most importantly, when you perform the prayer of need, you should feel confident that God will answer your prayer, but in the way that He Knows is best for you.

58 Arabic phrase for the "Companions of the Battle of Badr". Around 320 Muslims participated in the the Battle of Badr (March 624) which is the first major military victory led by the Prophet Muhammad (Peace be upon Him) that marked a turning point for the early Muslim community from a defensive stance toward one of stability and expansion.

children's room. He had a habit of performing morning prayers in the children's room. Fatih was sleeping in that room, Zeynep was in my bed. Soon Gokhan arrived to the bedroom after performing his morning prayer. When I saw him in front of me, I thought my heart was going to explode! He was wearing a suit, pure white. He went straight next to Zeynep who was sleeping in the bed, while I stood up and waited gently. He stroked our daughter's hair, kissed her, watched her with love and compassion in his eyes, and then he came up to me and stood right in front of me. I looked at him in tears. Yes, it was him! He was standing in front of me, and it was all real. I hugged him, crying, "Where have you been?" He hugged me tightly, and we just stood there for a while. I still couldn't believe it and kept saying, "Where have you been?! Why? Aren't you dead?" "No," he said in response to me "I'm not dead. They just told me not to be around for a while as a precaution. But I am nearby."

When we were crossing the Maritza river, I was more worried about my children than myself. I wouldn't mind if anything happened to me, but what if something were to happen to my children?! As we were on the shore of the Maritza, I felt Gokhan's presence with us and said quietly, "These are your son and daughter, too! We will pass through Maritza, come and protect your children!"

The Life and Legacy of Gokhan Acikkollu

Every now and then, I have been still receiving so many stories about Gokhan, even from people I do not know. Not long ago, I was informed about an incident that happened in a refugee camp in Europe. One of the brothers in Hizmet saw a vision in which Gokhan visited him in the camp room and covered him up with a blanket while he was sleeping. When he opened his eyes and saw Gokhan, his first reaction was, "But Brother, aren't you dead!?" Gokhan answered, quite surprised, "Why is everyone asking me this? I'm not dead, I'm on my duty!" When he was asked about that surveillance footage which was showing his last moments, Gokhan would say, "I got out of bed and approached those iron bars because Prophet Muhammad (Peace be upon Him) had visited me to give me a job: *'Our brothers and sisters will pass across the Aegean Sea and the Maritza River, and some of them will fall into the water meanwhile, your job is to save them!'*" According to that brother in the camp, Gokhan said that his new duty was to visit his brothers in Hizmet who were staying in refugee camps.

Another brother in Hizmet, who also was staying in the camps, saw Gokhan in his dream with another friend. Gokhan was waiting inside a school with a bundle of *"Sizinti"*[59] magazines. The entrances and exits of the

---

[59] *Sizinti* was a monthly culture, science, history, and religion magazine published by members of the Hizmet movement between 1979 and July 2016

building were sealed off by the police. His friend asked him "Brother, you're dead, what are you doing here?!" Gokhan responded, "No, I am not dead! I am on my duty! This is not the time to take a break!" When his friend asked "But how are you going to get through the cops now?" Gokhan did not even replied; he just walked towards the police officers and passed through them who could not see him.

There are dozens of visions and dreams like this. So many people, most of whom don't even know each other, can't be wrong about the same thing. I have resigned myself to the fact that Gokhan was indeed invited to the other world before us and he left. We will continue to live in this world until our time is up. Every individual will indeed die the way he has lived.

Gokhan had always desired two things when he was alive: One was to emigrate for the sake of Allah, the other was to die a martyr!

Both of his wishes came true, Allah's Will.

He emigrated to the Homeland!

---

in Turkey. The magazine promoted itself with the motto, "The magazine of love and tolerance." *Sızıntı* was closed down by the Turkish government on 27 July 2016.

The Life and Legacy of Gokhan Acikkollu

LIFE OF GOKHAN ACIKKOLLU IN CHRONOLOGICAL ORDER

1974   **Born in Istanbul**

1997   Graduated from Konya Selcuk University, Department of History.

1998   **Married Mumine Tulay Acikkollu.**

1999   **His son, Murat Fatih, was born.**

2002   Military service in Şemdinli, Hakkari.

2003   Started to work as principle in a middle school in Aksaray.

2006   Started to work in a learning center in Konya.

2009   **His daughter, Zeynep Munise, was born.**

2010   Appointed to Istanbul and started working at Doga College.

2012   Appointed to a public school in Gaziantep.

2013   Appointed to Umraniye Ataturk Anatolian Technical and Vocational High School.

July 22, 2016   **Suspended from his duty by a government decree-law**

July 23, 2016   **Detained.**

August 5, 2016   **Died in a detention cell.**

February 2, 2018   **Reinstated to his job**

PHOTOS

Tulay Acikkollu & Gokhan Acikkollu - 1998

Last Family Picture – July 17, 2016

Zeynep (daughter), Tulay (wife), unknown, unknown, Gokhan, Fatih (son)

Gokhan and Zeynep

The Life and Legacy of Gokhan Acikkollu

Tulay, Zeynep, Gokhan

Gokhan with his students

The Life and Legacy of Gokhan Acikkollu

Tulay

The Life and Legacy of Gokhan Acikkollu

ARTICLES IN THE TURKISH PENAL CODE WHICH ARE VIOLATED IN THE CASE OF GOKHAN ACIKKOLLU

ARTICLE 7- (1) *A person may neither be punished nor subject to a security measure for an act which does not constitute an offense according to the law in force at the time of commission of the offense. Also, one may neither be punished nor subject to a security measure for an act which does not constitute an offense according to the law which is put into force after the commission of the offense. Where a punishment or security precautions of that sort is imposed, its execution and legal consequences are spontaneously abrogated.*

(2) *Where there are differences between provisions of the law in force at the time of commission of the offense and the provisions of the law subsequently put into force, the law which is in favor of the perpetrator is applied and enforced.*

However, all of the people who were detained and arrested after the so-called July 15 coup plot, including Gokhan Acikkollu, were dismissed from their jobs, subjected to isolation, and even deprived of their freedom - which is considered to be the most fundamental right of a person - due to acts that were not considered a crime under the Turkish Penal Code. Tens of thousands of individuals were trialed in "July 15 related" courts, most of them were found guilty and sentenced for imprisonment, for the acts which did not constitute a criminal offense under the law in force at the time it was committed, or even at the time of those trials. Some of those so-called "criminal offenses" were being subscribed to the best-selling newspaper in Turkey, Zaman, which was in circulation since 1986; having an account in Bank Asya, which was one of the biggest banks in Turkey since 1996; and choosing the schools affiliated with Hizmet Movement for your children to attend. İnviting your friends to your house or visiting them in their houses on a regular basis was also considered a crime.

ARTICLE 20- (1) *Criminal responsibility arises from a private wrong. No one can be held responsible for another person's act.*

Using the so-called July 15 coup plot as an excuse, thousands of people were detained and arrested, who had nothing to do with the coup. Innocent citizens were declared traitors overnight, even though no elements of crime were present, regarding to participating in the coup or any other crime. Gokhan Açıkkollu was tortured to death for a crime he did not commit.

ARTICLE 21- (1) *In order to consider an act as an offense, a crime has to be intended by the offender. Malice is an intention to cause harm being aware of the legal consequences of the crime* *defined in the laws.*

Although thousands of people during the trials related to the so-called July 15 coup plot stated that they have joined the Hizmet movement only for religious and philanthropic purposes, the judges and prosecutors, under the heavy influence of the Turkish government, declared them terrorists. They had neither intended to commit a crime nor the act they committed was considered as a crime in the Penal Code.

ARTICLE 76- (1) *Execution of any one of the following acts under a plan against members of national, racial or religious groups with the intention of destroying the complete or part of the group, creates the legal consequence of an offense defined as genocide.*

a) Voluntary manslaughter

b) To act with the intention of giving severe corporal or spiritual injury,

c) To impose conditions that make survival of complete or part of the group members impossible,

d) To impose that prevent births in the group,

e) To transfer minors of a group to another group,

(2) *A person who commits the offense of genocide is sentenced to heavy imprisonment.*

Those police officers, prosecutors, judges, government officials, and politicians who have taken a role in the brutal treatment of hundreds of thousands of people are the perpetrators of the crime of GENOCIDE and will be tried when the rule of law comes back to Turkey. There is no statute of limitations for these crimes. Hundreds of thousands of innocent people were dismissed from their jobs by government decree-laws, on the grounds of their affiliation with the Hizmet movement. The Turkish government acted with the intention of giving severe corporal or spiritual injury to those people. The Turkish government did not allow them to work in any other job, anywhere in Turkey. Moreover, their passports were canceled by the Turkish government, so they were not allowed to leave Turkey, either. People were condemned to starvation and poverty. Even those who helped the needy families were tried for aiding and abetting terrorism. Turkish government has imposed conditions that make survival of hundreds of thousands of Hizmet movement members impossible. Turkish government has committed GENOCIDE. The perpetrators of this crime will be held accountable and put in trial, sooner or later.

ARTICLE 77- (1) *Execution of any one of the following acts systematically under a plan against a sector of a community for political, philosophical, racial or religious reasons, creates the legal* *consequence of an offense against humanity.*

a) Voluntary manslaughter,

b) To act with the intention of giving injury to another person,

c) Torturing, infliction of severe suffering, or forcing a person to live as a slave,

d) To restrict freedom,

e) To make a person to be subject to scientific researches/tests

f) Sexual harassment, child molestation,

g) Forced pregnancy

h) Forced prostitution

Hundreds of thousands of innocent people have been arrested within the scope of Hizmet movement prosecutions. Their lives have been attempted, they have been beaten, injured, and exposed to systemic torture. The perpetrators will be held accountable before the law for their CRIMES AGAINST HUMANITY, without the statute of limitations. There is enough evidence and witnesses for the fact that Gokhan Acikkollu was tortured to death. In addition, he was not given the medication he used regularly.

ARTICLE 94-(1) *Any public officer who causes severe bodily or mental pain, or loss of conscious or ability to act, or dishonors a person, is sentenced to imprisonment from three years to twelve years.*

Every person who has been detained, arrested, and put on trial within the scope of Hizmet movement prosecutions, has been tortured. Torture can take many forms. Torture can be physical, taking the form of physical assaults or beatings, or electric shocks. Torture can be psychological, or mental, where victims are exposed to loud noise, or solitary confinement, for long periods of time. Torture can also be sexual, involving rape and/or humiliation. While psychological torture may not leave any lasting physical damage, it can result in similar levels of permanent mental damage to its victims.

ARTICLE 109-(1) *Any person who unlawfully restricts the freedom of a person by preventing him from traveling or living in a place is sentenced to imprisonment from one year to five years.*

(2) *If a person uses physical power or threat or deception to perform an act or during the commission of offense, then he is sentenced to imprisonment from two years to seven years.*

(3) *In case of commission of this offense;*

a) By use of a weapon,

b) Jointly by a group of persons,

c) By virtue of a public office,

d) By undue influence based on public office,

e) Against antecedents, descendants or spouse,

f) Against a child or a person who cannot protect himself due to corporal or spiritual disability,

The punishment imposed according to the above subsections is increased by one-fold.

(4) *If this offense results with gross economical loss of the victim, the offender additionally is imposed a punitive fine up to one thousand days.*

(5) *In case of commission of offense with sexual intent, the punishments to be imposed according to the above subsections are increased by one-half.*

(6) *The provisions relating to felonious injury are additionally applied in case of commission of aggravated form of this offense which creates the consequences of felonious injury.*

After the so-called 15 July coup plot, the crime of Deprivation of Freedom was committed by the Turkish government against hundreds of thousands of Hizmet movement members. The judges and prosecutors, under the heavy influence of the Turkish government, committed the crime of unlawfully restricting the freedom of innocent people, for the acts of those innocent people which did not constitute a criminal offense under the law in force at the time it was committed, or even during the time of court trials.

ARTICLE 4- (1) *Ignorance of the criminal laws may not be an excuse.*

While it is unacceptable for even an ordinary citizen not to know the penal code, it will definitely not be acceptable for the pro-government judges and prosecutors when the time comes and they try to take shelter behind statements such as "We had trusted the government" or "How could we know?"

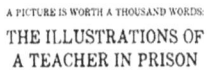

AST PUBLISHING

Hafza Girdap is the executive director and the spokesperson for AST (Advocates of Silenced Turkey) and the founding member of Set Them Free platform who works for the women's rights violated particularly in Turkey. Girdap is also a Ph.D. candidate in Women's and Gender Studies at Stony Brook University, New York. Girdap has a B.A. and M.A. in English Language and Literature. Her research areas are human rights and women's status in Muslim contexts, specifically the integration and adaptation of Muslim immigrant women while redefining their cultural identities. Girdap is interested in analyzing the lives of Muslim women regarding the challenges they face within their own cultures, before, during, and after conflicts. Her doctoral research focuses on self-identification and the gendered representation and reshaping of Muslim women who grew up in Islamic cultures but resettled to Western cultures. Her research takes an intersectional framework. In addition to her professional human rights work and academic studies, Girdap conducts researches at ECPS's gender program (European Center for Populism Studies https://www.populismstudies.org/about-us/programs/gender/) as a nonresident research associate.

While carrying out her research, Girdap includes the voices of female survivors of conflict by examining the coping mechanisms used by these women to manage new and existing challenges, including social discrimination, oppression, violations of basic rights, etc. She studies how they manage when facing these challenges within different contexts, i.e. their own countries, refugee camps, and new settlements. Girdap has been living in the US since July 2016 as a result of political persecution she faced in her native Turkey. Since settling in the States, her research interests expanded and she has become much more involved in women's rights movements. Accordingly, she has participated in many programs and delivered speeches about the status of women in Muslim societies. Girdap has been organizing and speaking at UNGA and UN CSW panels for three years, with a focus on women's matters and experiences. She also mentors youth in the hope that they will become involved in these events as researchers and speakers. As having a personal motto in her life which is "Let Dreams Lead You!", Girdap is running online global bookclubs on Instagram where she also makes live interviews concerning women and youth empowerment. Hafza, with her two daughters (18 and 13 years) and her husband, is living on Long Island, New York.

MINA LEYLA

Born in a small town but grew up with big dreams.

Told stories as a child, wanted to be a journalist from a young age.

Was the president of the "reading club" at school, always loved and read books, and wrote some, too.

Got upset like everybody else, made mistakes, disappointed. But got to know people who beautified her story and collected many memories.

Took interest in stories, true stories or the ones likely to happen…

Wanted to be a journalist but studied "radio and television."

Played the leading role in her story, reached her dreams, thanked God.

Began her career by putting her foot on the first rung of the ladder, worked as a reporter.

Wrote countless scenarios…worked as an editor for five years…was a source of pride for her parents.

Loved the Fall season, the flowers, the olive trees, Turkish coffee, and Istanbul…

In the battle of the oppressor and the oppressed, she took sides with the oppressed.

She couldn't love Istanbul anymore when the truth and lies were all twisted together, when friends turned into enemies, and all the holy values became just a tool of politics.

Took as a guide the verse in the Quran: "Was God's earth not wide enough for you to emigrate in it?" So, she looked at the world map.

Became an immigrant…and a refugee.

Cried some, missed a lot…but most of all, observed the people and events around her…she tried…and prayed…

Reset herself to zero…

Met other refugees, listened to their stories, and stopped feeling sorry for herself.

…and so, she has set a new goal in her life:

"To be human first!"